Land Acknowledgment

The 3rd Thing is located at the southern tip of the Salish Sea on the unceded land of the Medicine Creek Treaty Tribes: the Nisqually, Puyallup, Steilacoom, Squaxin, S'Homamish, Stehchass, T'Peeksin, Squi-aitl and the Sa-heh-wamish. As part of our work to create a culture of intimacy, accountability and radical imagination, we acknowledge the violent legacy of settlement and ongoing colonialism and commit to cultivating restorative relationships with Indigenous communities and with the land.

In support of truth-telling and reconciliation, and with the belief that a book can be a liberated and liberatory space that travels through time and across borders, each of our 2020 Cohort authors shares their pages with Melissa Bennett, an Indigenous writer whose work serves as an invitation to listen more closely and to more voices.

Melissa Bennett

Melissa Bennett, M.Div. (Umatilla/Nez Perce/Sac & Fox/Anishinaabe) is a writer, storyteller, story listener, educator, and spiritual care provider living as a guest on Medicine Creek Treaty Tribes land. Melissa is interested in story as medicine, especially its ability to heal historical trauma among Indigenous communities. The series of poems printed at the front of The 3rd Thing's 2020 titles is meant to reflect the ways in which our lives are intertwined with the stories and memories of our ancestors and our descendants. They bring the past, present, and future together through place, people, traditions, culture, and faith practices. These poems ask where we have been and where we belong in the story of our own becoming.

Church

by Melissa Bennett

and because

the candles

aren't working

and the tears

of the old ones

stain the floor

I crawl

into the dark

with the medicine

cedar	rose	huckleberry	sage	salmon	water
talátat	tamsásnim	siwey	cemítx	qémqem	tánat	chuush

I cleanse

the grief

of my womb

there

.

THERE MUST BE
HAPPY ENDINGS

The 3rd Thing

editors@the3rdthing.press

Bookseller & academic distribution
is handled by Small Press Distribution, spdbooks.org.
Support the press and writer with your individual purchases
through the3rdthing.press.

Cover & book design by Anne de Marcken
Cover image, Juan Alonso-Rodríguez
Author photo, Maggie Hall Photography

Typeset in Caslon, Century Gothic and Origin Super Condensed

Printed in the United States of America by
Spencer Printing.

ISBN: 978-1-7344071-1-2

LCCN: 2020931410

FIRST EDITION

2 4 6 8 9 7 5 3

THERE MUST BE HAPPY ENDINGS

ON A THEATER OF OPTIMISM & HONESTY

Megan Sandberg-Zakian

3

The 3rd Thing, Olympia, Washington

Contents

Ladies and gentleman, don't feel let down:
We know this ending makes some people frown.
We had in mind a sort of golden myth
Then found the finish had been tampered with.
Indeed it is a curious way of coping:
To close the play, leaving the issue open...
What's your answer? Nothing's been arranged.
Should men be better? Should the world be changed?
Or just the Gods? Or ought there to be none?
We for our part feel well and truly done.
There's only one solution that we know:
That you should now consider as you go
What sort of measures you would recommend
To help good people to a happy end.
Ladies and gentlemen, in you we trust:
There must be happy endings, must, must, must!

Epilogue to *The Good Person of Szechwan* by Bertolt Brecht

There Must Be Happy Endings

During our wedding planning, my now-wife and I had a disagreement about including the words "till death do us part" in our vows. I said: This is what it means to get married! You stay together until one of you dies! She said: Absolutely not! Why should we stay together until death if it isn't working?

It's likely that what she actually said was something very nuanced and reasonable—something like, "Getting married means you're willing to work at being on a shared path together. Sometimes people change, and sometimes paths diverge."—but what I heard was "Not every marriage has a happy ending."

In Homer's *Odyssey*—which I was somehow never assigned in school and so had the pleasure of reading, of my own free will, as an adult—Penelope dismantles her weaving each night, as a ruse to postpone a second marriage and thus remain faithful to her absent husband Odysseus. While Odysseus travels the hero's journey, facing monsters inside and outside of himself, Penelope waits at home—raveling and unraveling, to defer the ending, to preserve the possibility of happiness.

I've always liked Penelope's story, but I began to deeply

empathize with her while attempting to write this book. I am a theater director. I have never written a book before. As I've raveled and unraveled these essays, I've felt how painful it is to unmake something I so carefully and recently made. I have seen how easily the thread is tangled, how tedious the weaving and unweaving can be, how tempting it is to turn away from the loom and surrender—to a pint of Cherry Garcia, or, I suppose, to one of your 108 suitors. I have seen how desperately I crave a happy ending, whether to a book or a life's story.

But an ending doesn't *have* to be happy to be satisfying. A good ending, happy or not, draws a line around the experience of story hearing and telling. It picks the story up, holds it in its hands, and offers it out, whole. It gives us the opportunity for a collective breath. A good ending is honest: a boundary we can feel, the knowable edge of a reliable container. It is a ritual threshold between story and not-story.

In my theater-going life, I've seen attempts to subvert the ending: installation performances where we can choose when and how the experience begins and ends, plays with no curtain call, which leave us sitting in tense silence for long minutes until uncertain applause begins, plays that turn up the music, pull us into the aisles, and transform the performance into a dance party. But these are just different kinds of endings, and in all these cases, as an audience member, I knew when the show was over.

As a director, I often find the ending image of a play first. I'll daydream about the ending, replaying it decadently, guiltily, like a child who is only eating dinner because she knows what's for dessert.

It's not strictly true that I've never written a book before. Every year at Madrona Elementary school during the annual read-a-thon, we got to write a book—you could tell it was a book and not a story because the handwritten pages were spiral bound with a laminated cover. In fourth grade, my book was called *Everything Always Comes Out In The End*. It was based on the story of my unlikely friendship with Amy Swift, who, to my despair, had moved away at the end of third grade. I remember conceiving of the ending, in which the narrator, who had been brave and vulnerable enough to reach out to a new friend only to lose her to California, was rewarded for her open-heartedness by receiving overtures of friendship from not one but *two* other girls.

The title of the book felt both aspirational and true. I *did* want everything to come out in the end, and I thought it probably could. I loved stories that offered triumph over adversity, unlikely reunions, last minute rescues. I rooted for happy endings. I believed they must be possible.

—

When I graduated from college, I moved to New York City

and registered to vote at my new address on Hudson Street. On election day, my neighborhood polling place couldn't find my name, so I rode my teal-blue Schwinn down to the Board of Elections on Varick Street. I was filling out forms in a lobby on the 17th floor when a jetliner dropped out of a perfect azure sky and flew into a building twenty blocks south. A man next to me kept repeating, "My nephew works in there. He works on the 90th floor." We were close enough to make out dark forms leaping from the upper floors of the building. As I pedaled back up Hudson towards my apartment, I saw hundreds of people lining the streets convulse in unison, crying out. I realized later that must have been the moment when the first tower fell. I watched the second tower collapse from the roof of my building.

It felt like the end.

I was altered by that encounter with the world's violent unpredictability, which I'd previously understood only in the abstract. Before that day, I saw tragedy, violence, hate as blemishes in an essentially compassionate universe, as aberrations that must be resisted, fought against and overcome for the sake of our beautiful world. After, I saw them as pervasive. I saw the fundamental chaos in the lives of the nine-year-olds in my playwriting class, who were often at the mercy of brutal public systems. I heard it in the sobs of my roommate through the wall at night and in the voices of Baghdadi teenagers that came over the radio in the months and years after my country invaded theirs. I looked into the faces of strangers on the street and recognized my own devastation. Now I understood that *this was the world*: unjust, irrational, cruel.

But September 11 was not the end, at least not for me. Both before and after that day, I made theater. I still make theater. Sometimes—often—it seems like a deeply inadequate response to a world of terror and chaos. But I strive to meet that world with my full and honest attention. In the collision between that striving and the whisper of my childhood longing—*please, let everything work out*—I find myself again considering happy endings.

What can a happy ending offer us?—and, now, I mean an honestly happy ending, not a dishonest one. Not one that papers over reality with false cheer, but one that earns its happiness with full truth, with clear-eyed presence. That acknowledges the irrationality of the human heart, the infinite unavoidable harms to self and others, the violence of the systems we've made to support us but that fall so short, the maddening complexity of things that should be clear.

Is this kind of happy ending even possible? One that gives us a compassionate space where grief and loss can co-exist with hope and joy? One that offers us an alleviation, a space of relief, where the weight of the world's terror abates momentarily? Perhaps it could act as a restorative, a tonic that refreshes and rebalances? And then, too, it would need to open up the space to rejoice, to be washed with pure delight, wouldn't it? In a world where everything changes, in an ever-expanding universe, can a container the size of a theater and the shape of two hours be big enough to hold all this?

I've tried to retain Penelope's faith that happy endings are not arrived at inevitably, but made, and re-made, and re-made. She perseveres—in the face of possible violence to her person, rejoicing in hope long after there is reasonable cause for it, imagining reunion when others assume it is impossible. Faced with forces—both human and divine—that seek to overpower her, she courageously, optimistically, persistently, continues to make her own story. She reminds me that there is only one way I can know for certain there will never be a happy ending: if I do not persist in imagining one.

And still I wonder: how do I reconcile my desire for hope and possibility, connection and transformation, with an authentic witnessing of darkness and despair, hate and violence? In the face of an enormously unjust and chaotic history and present, is it acceptable—is it ethical?—to believe in the happy ending? Is it possible to be both honest *and* hopeful? Although I write from the viewpoint of someone making theater, I believe that this balancing act is one that all sensitive human beings must at some point attend to. It is the essential question of how to, as Walter Lippmann wrote, "live forward in the midst of complexity."

In the midst of preparing this book for publication, I went on my first week-long silent meditation retreat. The teachers kept emphasizing that the work of being truly present in the here and now, being with *what is*, is a process of constantly remembering and forgetting. We have moments of clarity and insight that seem to transform us. Then we become preoccupied with the small tasks of daily life, and we forget that we were transformed. Then, we turn back towards the present, we practice, we breathe, and we remember. Everything changes. We forget, we remember. Over and over.

I saw this so clearly as I roamed the surrounding farmland in between meditation sits. Twin baby goats were born, and in a week went from collapsed and helpless, to head-butting the chickens. I fed their mother some grass through the fence. Her breath was warm and her tongue gentle as she took it from my hand. Near the grape arbor, a group of caterpillars clustered together on a branch, while other caterpillars wove a white silk enclosure around them. There was a dead toad on the path. Then, one night, a large and very alive toad hopped out of the woods and stopped for a long time to stare at me, its throat pulsing rapidly, a shimmering cloud of small flying insects between us.

I was vibrating all over. I felt the edges of my body pulsing, melting. The moon rose, smelling of honeysuckle and, for some reason, peanut butter. My feet—or someone's feet—walked on the damp grass. I felt I might be in a dream, dreaming myself. I might go to sleep that night and wake up gone—some part of me in everything, but the shape of me dissolved, like a sugar cube in a lake.

If the end were to come now, it would be a happy ending.

But I did not dissolve, that I could tell. I appeared to come home in the same physical form as I'd left.

My wife was on a work trip so the house was empty. I walked— slowly—from room to room. We live on the third floor of an old New England triple-decker. Spring sunlight filtered through the branches of the fir trees that fill our small front yard. The owner of the building on our left had for some time refused to cut down a large and very dead tree in his driveway. This tree, right outside our living room windows, provided endless hours of speculation and dread. Every time there was a big storm, we were terrified that it would come crashing down. After the last blizzard, during which several large branches had fallen, thankfully damaging nothing except our recycling bin, I had made yet another complaint to the city and to the landlord, neither of whom replied.

Now, in the spring, the red-bellied woodpeckers were loving this tree. A pair of starlings was flying into a hole in the trunk with worms to feed their babies. And I could see that, directly facing the living room, a peach-colored dove had built her nest in the crook of a dead branch and was sitting, serenely, atop it.

I got home on a Friday. On Monday, a landscaping company pulled up to the house next door and began to unload. I watched, first with curiosity and then with horror, as they prepared to finally remove this hazardous old tree. Their chain saws buzzed. They prepared by tying ropes around various branches, attaching pulleys, calculating. A man ascended in a small metal cabin on the arm of a machine. From the living room, I locked eyes with the dove on her nest. She sat, tensely, even as the sawdust began to fly around her. The starlings, alarmed, flew around in circles. They might have been screaming, but I couldn't hear them over the machine's roar.

It was very, very loud.

I backed away from the window. I thought of leaving the house, but that felt both disloyal and cowardly. I couldn't watch, but I couldn't leave. I sat, quietly, at our dining room table, for hours, while the tree, and everything in it, came down in pieces. Once the pieces were down, the landscaping team fed them to a wood-chipping machine and drove them away. The street was quiet again. I crept back to the window. A pair of doves and a pair of starlings flew in confused zig zags around the yard.

Was this, perhaps, the end?

I felt like it might be. I was so nauseous I could barely stand.

The tree had been removed at my insistence. The baby birds had been fed to a wood chipper because I asked to be safe.

Maybe, I thought, there is only a finite amount of peace. Is the world always rebalancing in this way—yin for yang, hard for soft, dark for light? Does safety here mean peril over there? Does comfort there mean hardship over here? Maybe happiness is a zero sum game.

In the decade since I began writing these essays, I've moved to a different city, built a thriving career, gotten married, gotten sick, lost people I loved, lost my car in a flash flood. The world, too, has been swept with altering events. It has been made and unmade. It is now 2019, and when I tell colleagues the subject of my book, they sigh in recognition. They say it is a book we need right now. I think, but do not say, that this is a book I have needed over and over in my life, at moments spanning radically different political regimes and personal experiences. The questions in these essays are not questions for times that are worse or times that are better. They are persistent questions. I have asked and answered them differently over the years. They are questions about the stories we tell ourselves about ourselves.

I am writing this, my first (adult) book, in the dining room of my middle class home in a gentrified neighborhood of a progressive city in a wealthy nation. Destruction—of baby birds, of the planet and its inhabitants—is done in my name, with my collusion, for my safety, for the warmth of my home and the speed of my travel.

I'm also the grand-child and great grand-child of Armenian and Jewish immigrants. I have twentieth-century genocides on both sides of my heritage. My spouse is African American. She is the great-grand-child of enslaved persons. We are both queer women. When we scroll past the news side by side, it can feel like there is quite literally no part of who we are together that is not under attack, that somebody does not want to obliterate.

We suffer. We are implicated in the suffering of others. We can seek to anesthetize our suffering; we can refuse to see the harm we have done. Or we can try to step forward, to show up for our own suffering, to be present to the suffering we have abetted, to seek remedy.

Looking directly at terrible things is hard, but harder still is looking at the part of yourself that understands them. It's easy to say, "that doesn't make sense." It's very hard to say, "I can find the impulse for that violence in myself. That thing of darkness I acknowledge mine."

It is winter now. The stump outside our window cannot be seen—it is covered with snow—but I know it is there. The wind blows hard, slightly shaking the old plaster walls. I can hear my wife, in her office, singing.

I am glad the tree is down, that she is safe.

As I cut these essays from the loom—happily—I know that this is only a book-shaped moment, the length of ten essays. The way I answer these questions has changed in the writing of them, and will certainly change again. Everything changes. I will remember, and forget, and remember. I know enough to understand this isn't the ending. But at least now, I have begun.

The Old Dark Cloud Comes Over Me

Summer was like your house: you knew
where each thing stood.
Now you must go out into your heart
as onto a vast plain. Now
the immense loneliness begins.

– Rilke

It was October, and I was eight years old, about to be nine. I have an especially clear memory of riding to school on those slightly damp autumn mornings, breathing foggy spots onto the bus window, thinking about how this part of my life—the single digit part—would soon be over forever. The transition into double digits felt significant, both interesting and foreboding.

It was only my second month ever of riding the bus to school. In the fifteen minutes between when I let go of my dad's hand and climbed the few steep bus stairs, and when we reached my friend Kate's stop in Ballard, I sat alone—legs swinging against the green vinyl seat, nose pressed against the rattling window, breathing in the outdoor smell of my coat collar and the burnt-toast of bus heat. I mentally reviewed the other ages I had been, as if from a great distance. I remembered being four and having to wear a cast after I broke my ankle jumping off the top of a dresser. I remembered being five, running around the house in circles screaming, playing "three little pigs" with Kate. I remembered being six, lining up all my stuffed animals on the bed with my new infant brother in the middle because he was the same size as they were, and I remembered taking a picture of the line-up with my new Polaroid camera.

I remembered being seven, sitting on the steps of our old house in Fremont, watching shiny black beetles march across our front walk, on their way from one part of the lawn to another. Usually the beetles just scurried by, but this once there was one that seemed interested in me, crawling over the twigs I offered to it, eventually resting near my foot. Almost nine, I recalled the feeling of being seven, the sunlight on the back of my neck, the pleasure of being in company with a small, strange creature, the sweet, dark smell of beetle. When my mother came outside, I asked her if I could keep the beetle as a pet. She examined it and told me the beetle was dead and I needed to come in for dinner. I did go in, but I didn't quite believe her. The beetle didn't feel dead to me. I looked for it in the morning, but it was gone.

Though that had seemed like proof to seven-year-old me that my friend the beetle was still alive, almost-nine-year-old me was not so sure. I could feel a different truth approaching.

I remember exactly when I began to understand that the world's unspeakable beauty was matched only by its unspeakable horror. It was just an ordinary day of soccer practice that it happened. My soccer team was called The Unicorns. In my memory of this day, I am wearing my shiny blue and gold uniform, although I'm not sure why I would have been wearing my uniform at practice. There was a team meeting about something—I don't recall what—and everyone got very upset. The group of players and coaches and parents, standing in the middle of the field, began to argue. I remember feeling filled with melancholy, wandering away from the group, and sitting on the bleachers. I watched the Unicorns and their adult guardians gesticulating wildly at each other in the middle of the field. Their conflict felt unbearably violent. I lay down flat on the cold metal and looked up at the beautiful sky, darkening blue with a glow of apricot at the edges, framed by a lattice of almost-bare branches. The world is terrible, I realized. And here I am in the middle of it. I thought about all the things I'd heard of that were bad: nuclear bombs, greenhouse gases, starving Ethiopians. I remember that when my dad came to pick me up, I was crying so hard he thought I was injured. I had to explain, through sobs, that I was crying not for myself, but for the world.

On my ninth birthday, I got the one thing I really wanted, a Cabbage Patch Kid with auburn cornsilk hair named Disa Eve Gilberta. I felt lucky. I *was* lucky. People said I was smart and pretty and good at soccer, and I believed them. When another child at school behaved badly, my mother would point out possible contributing factors: his parents were divorced, she had a learning disability. Having all the advantages of health and comfort, I had no excuse for boredom, sadness, or underachievement. "After all," Mom would say, "if you can't be happy, who can?"

I mulled this over alongside the new knowledge from that day on the soccer field. The world was full of bad things *and* I was supposed to be happy. I was nine and knew I would someday be ten, and so on, and already there was a strange dread in my belly, a fear that I would not be able to follow the edict implicit in my mother's logic.

Sometime after my ninth birthday, I formed a new belief that integrated my mother's doctrine and my own experience: it was not okay to be sad for myself, but it *was* okay—even laudable—to be sad for the world. Using my sadness as fuel to save others allowed me to indulge the feeling of grief inside me and still be good, and lucky, and smart, and happy. I could be the kind of girl I was supposed to be, *and* I could make the world a better place. I could make a difference.

I started with the dolphins. I knew from the mailings Greenpeace sent to our house that they were dying, because of tuna. I formed a theater company, consisting of my three year-old brother and myself, called "The S-Z Stars." Every time someone came to our house, The S-Z Stars offered a benefit performance, gathering guests in the living room for a brief, enthusiastic program. Little Eric had composed a five-line poem called "Hit a Ball" that always went over well. I sang some songs, gave a speech about dolphins, and distributed S-Z Stars business cards handwritten in magic marker. Afterwards, we collected a quarter from everyone present. After several months, I turned over all the cash to my father, who wrote a check to Greenpeace for twelve dollars and change. I sealed it into one of the postage-paid envelopes that came in the dolphin mailings and sent it off, proud.

This early experiment in philanthropy started me down the road I would follow into my professional life—a sense that my work as a director and producer of theater could respond to, and even combat, the injustices of the world around me. I embraced a stance of what Jill Dolan calls "militant optimism"—a persistent belief that theater can model utopian social relationships and reaffirm hope and faith. Like Dolan, I believed live performance could be transformative for audiences and communities, offering "not iterations of what *is*, but transformative doings of what *if*." This militant optimism felt like a magical shield, allowing me to venture into dark places and find meaning, purpose, grace.

As a director, I was drawn to projects that dealt with difficult subjects with sensitivity and grace, plays that made the audience cry but also left them with a tiny, warm spark. Every few years I would read a new play that grabbed me by the shoulders, yelling "Yes! We understand each other! We were made for each other!" So it was with a script by Lydia Diamond that had been developed at Steppenwolf Theatre in Chicago; I was to direct the second production at the Underground Railway Theater in Cambridge. The play, *Harriet Jacobs*, was freely adapted by Diamond from Jacobs's 1861 slave narrative *Incidents in the Life of a Slave Girl*. It traced Jacobs's extraordinary life: her childhood in Edenton, North Carolina, her persecution as a teenager by her master and her attempts to avoid his assault, her audacious false escape where she pretended to flee North but actually remained hidden in her grandmother's shed—for seven years—so that she could watch her children grow up through a tiny peep-hole… and finally, her actual escape to the North and her eventual reunion with her children.

Jacobs's story is extraordinary and *Harriet Jacobs* is a wonderful play; I felt both the thrill and the heavy responsibility of achieving a production that did justice to its complexity and power. I read and re-read all of the research materials, over-prepared for every rehearsal. I wanted to capture the triumphant force of Jacobs's life in the vessel of this production. I wanted to make audiences feel as inspired and moved as I felt by her story. In our rehearsal room, we often sat around a six-foot white plastic table, the kind with the foldable legs. Lydia had described Jacobs's hiding place, a crawlspace under the roof of her grandmother's porch, as "about the size of the space under a large dining table." During rehearsals, I was sometimes momentarily paralyzed as I looked at the space under our white plastic table, crowded with backpacks and the feet of actors. *Seven years.*

Lydia was making changes to the script throughout the rehearsal process. In particular, we struggled with the ending. The last scene was a moving farewell between Harriet and her grandmother as Harriet prepared, after her long confinement, to stow away on a ship headed North. The scene ended with a monologue where Harriet directly addressed the audience, briefly describing the rest of the life she would find after this escape. Then the stage direction:

> *Ensemble members have gathered around her and have begun singing a hopeful, rousing spiritual. It is not a celebration... there is rather the conviction of one who will survive, the satisfaction of one who will tell her story... She walks upstage into the deep-blue sky of the future. Lights fade on all. End of play.*

We were having trouble striking the right tone for this final moment. I spent rehearsal breaks with my lighting and scenic designers, brainstorming solutions that would allow the ending to lift off with that final stage direction's sense of somber affirmation and forward movement.

The night before we started technical rehearsals, I went over and over my script as snow flurries began to swirl outside. I couldn't seem to catch my breath. At midnight, I walked through a blizzard to the Mt. Auburn Hospital Emergency Room and told them I was concerned that I had a pulmonary embolism. They took a chest x-ray and gave me fluids. The doctor suggested that I might just be very anxious. I wanted to tell him that it was reasonable to be anxious if you couldn't figure out the end of the play, but I didn't.

The next morning, the storm was over, but when I arrived to meet with the designers before tech, I found the building had lost power. In fact, the whole block was dark. The cast huddled in front of sunny windows in the greenroom, running lines and waiting for the lights to come back on. They didn't. We sent the actors home before the sun set. The next day, there was still no power, for all twelve hours of our scheduled rehearsal time. That night, a cast member got a call that her father had passed away. Another found out she needed emergency dental surgery.

On the train home from the dark theater, I cried, staring out at the blue, frozen suburbs. I thought about all the hours we'd missed. I wondered how to honor Harriet's memory without the rehearsal hours necessary to perfect the complex technical sequences in the second act, especially the ending. I wondered if the weekend's string of calamities meant that her spirit was unhappy with our production, with how we were telling her story. I felt we had proceeded with so much respect, treated her story with such reverence. What were we doing wrong? What could she object to?

I took a labored breath and reminded myself it was not a pulmonary embolism.

When I got home, there was an email from Kami Smith, the actress playing Harriet. She'd had some down time, thanks to the power outage, and decided to do a little research. She sent me a passage from a letter Jacobs wrote in 1867, when she returned for the first and only time to the place of her seven-year confinement. This was after the civil war was over, after abolition, and Jacobs wrote to Ednah Dow Cheney, a friend in the North:

> *I am sitting under the old roof, twelve feet from the spot*
> *where I suffered all the crushing weight of slavery. thank*
> *God, the bitter cup is drained of its last dreg... the change*
> *is so great I can hardly take it all in[.] I was born here,*
> *and amid all these new born blessings, the old dark cloud*
> *comes over me, and I find it hard to have faith in rebels.*

Although I'd pored over these letters for hours, the passage typed out in Kami's email felt new to me, as if I'd never really heard it before. Could this be Harriet Jacobs speaking, abolitionist heroine, brave and smart survivor? Were these her words even after she published her book, after slavery had ended, after she was reunited with her children?

What struck me in the re-encounter with this letter was its darkness, a darkness I'd missed or ignored before. Taking in this darkness made me understand some of Jacobs's other writing better. I could see that she struggled with feelings of despair and hopelessness, with shame and guilt, especially after she came North. I could see that faith, especially, was always a struggle for her, as she attempted to make sense of a God who would allow the horrors of slavery to continue; in spite of her belief in Christian ideals of charity and mercy, she was unable or unwilling to forgive the men and women who had participated in the enslavement of other human beings. I could see that even as I'd read and re-read Harriet's words, so shocked by her ordeal, so admiring of her triumph, I'd partially erased her.

This was something *I'd* done. It was not in Jacobs's and Diamond's texts, but in my interpretation of them. Lydia's play didn't ask for a sanitized heroine. Instead, it allowed for a woman who was by turns impatient, full of desire, angry, a bit of a smart-ass. And yes, she was also a person of enormous strength and tenacity. In her letter to Cheney, she went on to discuss the political, social and economic situation in Edenton in great detail. Even under the shadow of her dark cloud, she never disengaged with the larger struggle for justice. All of this was reflected in Lydia's text.

Kami's email suggested that the play's final monologue be set in the moment of the writing of this letter. While our previous approach had located the monologue, and Harriet's final exit, on the cusp of her escape from Edenton, this version would treat it as a more distant reflection. It was a risky, unstable moment to offer up as an ending—balancing both satisfaction and despair. In the letter, Harriet feels settled about the past, but "the old dark cloud" comes over her when she thinks about the future. She finds it difficult to have faith that the white people around her can truly change. And this sounded like the conversations our cast had been having for weeks around that plastic folding table, as precarious an exercise of imagination in Cambridge in 2010 as it had been in Edenton in 1867. It was an appropriate place to end our play.

The world's unspeakable beauty, matched only by its unspeakable horror.

Over the next week, before opening, Kami and I met every day before rehearsal. In those sessions, and in our work with the full cast, we went back through the play, finding places where we had scrubbed our heroine too clean. We put the texture back in. The play was better. The work didn't *feel* better to me—it felt more uncomfortable, less pretty—but I could see that it made the performance better. The story was being told more clearly, more honestly. There was more space for complexity. More space for the audience to feel.

I was very proud of that production of *Harriet Jacobs*. I especial-ly loved the ending, where I felt I had brought together the elements—Kami's performance, the music director's orchestra-tion of the haunting spiritual, and my design team's work on a striking final image—into something that elegantly achieved what Lydia was asking for. Near the end of the play, the planks were removed from the walls of the shed where Harriet had been confined, revealing rows of large glass mason jars filled with raw cotton. In the final moment, the jars lit up from within with tiny warm lights, turning the clouds of cotton into something otherworldly, and the ensemble placed a new jar in the center of the stage—an illuminated glass vessel with a small hardcover book in it. End of play.

We'd finally found the ending. But long after the show closed, the events of that tech weekend haunted me. It seemed to me that without the panic attacks and the lights going out, without Kami's email, I would have put a different production into the world—one that misrepresented both the complex history of the woman whose memory I wanted so badly to honor, and the complex present moment of my collaborators whom I so deeply loved and respected. I'd always assumed that my militant optimism was a magical shield that allowed me to descend, unscathed, into the darkness. But was I using my magic shield as self protection? As a way of resisting the reality and possibilities of that darkness? Did my commitment to work from a place of persistent hope dull my ability to be present with ideas, people and stories that were different from myself? Did it limit my ability to be present with my own darkness?

I felt that it did. It had. I was still that almost-nine-year old Unicorn, desperately sad for the world, standing next to it, vowing to change it.

Sentimentality, James Baldwin writes, "is the mark of dishonesty, the inability to feel; the wet eyes of the sentimentalist betray his aversion to experience, his fear of life, his arid heart; and it is always, therefore, the signal of secret and violent inhumanity, the mask of cruelty." Baldwin's harsh words were for Harriet Beecher Stowe, the white author of *Uncle Tom's Cabin* and a one-time hero of Jacobs's—until Jacobs wrote to Stowe for help publishing her life story and Stowe dismissively offered to mention Jacobs as an anecdote in her latest book. Jacobs, incensed, vowed to write the story without assistance, pointing out that her life's tale was powerful on its own merits and "needed no romance."

I contemplated my method of descending into the darkness with the shield of militant optimism. The entire time I was in the darkness, my goal was to either obliterate it (with light) or get the heck out of there (taking everyone else back to the light with me). I had decided I wanted to change a place without ever really seeing it. I traveled into a foreign land thinking that I knew more than its inhabitants, determined to make a heroic rescue. This role I had committed to playing was more missionary than moderator, more colonist than collaborator. By believing that my militant optimism could pierce through Harriet's "old dark cloud" and cast her story in a new light of hope, I denied the very center of her experience, and with it, any possibility for real contact. My hope had a directionality to it; it came from somewhere and wanted to go somewhere else. It had an agenda. My militant optimism was *too* militant.

I read and loved and directed other plays. None of them were comedies or romances. As always, I was drawn to work that asked for an encounter with painful subjects, tragic events, difficult questions. As I moved through these rehearsal processes, I was dogged by the old problem: When I come face to face with how terrible the world is, how do I respond? How do I locate myself in relationship to the darkness? And if I release my attachment to militant optimism, won't I spend every day sobbing on the bleachers, overwhelmed by the horror of the world around me?

"Now you must go out into your heart as onto a vast plain," Rilke wrote, "Now the immense loneliness begins."

Harriet Jacobs is buried, with her daughter Louisa, in Mt. Auburn Cemetery, right down the street from the Mt. Auburn Hospital ER and a few miles from the theater in Cambridge where we'd performed Lydia's play. While we were in rehearsal, Kami had taken the bus there to see her grave. I hadn't gone while we were working on the play. But after it was over, I began to visit regularly.

Mt. Auburn Cemetery was a good place for my questions. Founded by transcendentalists as the nation's first "garden cemetery," Mt. Auburn was intended to shift a fearful and punitive colonial-era attitude towards death and the afterlife. In lieu of an austere church graveyard, it has tranquil, meandering grounds—ponds and dells and hills and towers—which serve as both sacred resting place and pleasurable picnic spot. It is a place where the living and the dead can be together in quiet contemplation, where, as Judge Joseph Story said at the cemetery's 1831 consecration "we stand, as it were, upon the borders of two worlds."

I wish I could say I found some answers on the winding paths of Mt. Auburn Cemetery, but the truth is it took longer than that. I was stuck for awhile with the same questions. Sometimes I felt transformed, sometimes I felt defensive. Quite often I felt lonely. I'm not sure how to write about this. I kept feeling I had arrived somewhere and then realizing I had not. Have you ever taken a lengthy train trip in another country? You fall asleep and wake up, check out the window at unfamiliar landmarks, try to read signs in a language you only half understand. You keep wondering if you have missed your stop. It feels so long.

So, time passed. The relationship I was in ended. I went on a trip to Greece by myself and recited the epilogue to *Good Person of Szechwan* in the ancient theater of Epidaurus in the rain. Kami moved to Texas and gave up acting. People I loved died. Obama was re-elected. My friend Kate, with whom I used to play "three little pigs," had a baby, and so, to my delight, did my brother. My niece Charlotte could kick a soccer ball even before she could really walk. Charlotte is volatile and tender-hearted, so close to the bone of her own pain, so agitated with her own joy. Watching the extremes of life sweep through her small body, I feel a deep sense of recognition.

I think now of that little Unicorn in her shiny blue and yellow uniform, sobbing on the bleachers until her father came to collect her. Perhaps she cried because she knew that her health and wealth and comfort did not protect her from playing out her part in the world's secret and violent inhumanity. Perhaps she grieved the darkness inside as much as the darkness outside. But hers were not the wet eyes of Baldwin's sentimentalist.

Adults, I'd thought, were organized, rational, right. But on the soccer field that day I understood that they were no more right than I was, which is to say—not at all. The world flickered and darkened. I felt the chaos of not-knowing, asking me to step into it. As I shrank back, I saw an alternative to that terrifying complexity: the possibility that there was a right side and a wrong side and I could choose which one to be on.

I chose a side—fighting for something good.

It was not a choice born from sentimental violence. It sprang from a seed of deep empathy, a flash of sudden understanding about the nature of things. But it was also a choice born out of fear, that locked me for years in prison of my own optimism.

I can see this in Charlotte: how terrifying it is to face the world's unwanted possibilities, how comforting it is to believe in your own righteousness. I can see how badly she needs me to hold all of her. She is not always happy. She is not always good. I feel how necessary it is to leave space for her rage, her aggression, her despair.

My mother was right about the beetle, of course. Though at age seven my child's logic easily ducked the painful truth I wasn't ready to face, at age almost-nine, it was starting to come into focus. My response to the dawning realization that I lived in a world that included dead beetles was to crusade against the injustices of such a world—with enough effort, these problems could be fixed; surely beetles, dolphins, Unicorns and everyone's parents could all live in harmony.

My strategy for reckoning with a world full of unwanted possibilities—vanquish the darkness with my compulsory happiness!—had remarkable staying power. What I discovered working on *Harriet Jacobs* was that this strategy was insufficient.

I owe Harriet—and Charlotte—and myself—more than my happiness. I want to be available to my dissatisfaction, my anxiety, my grief, my despair; I want to live in this world fully, to be the kind of aunt I want to be, to make the kind of theater I want to make—the kind Jill Dolan believes in, and I believe in too, that reaffirms hope and faith and offers us a vision of another possible world, a transformative vision of *what if*.

—

It is the final day of rehearsal for our site-specific production of Thornton Wilder's *Our Town*. Mt. Auburn Cemetery is interested in using performance as a way of activating the landscape and allowing visitors to see the grounds in a new way. So our plan is to perform the first two acts of Wilder's masterpiece—"Daily Life" and "Love and Marriage"—in the quaint Story Chapel, and then travel with the audience down into Hazel Dell to play the third act—"Death and Eternity"—among the gravestones.

It is one of those brilliant New England fall days and we are rehearsing Act Three, one of my favorite stretches in all of American dramatic literature—the end of Emily's funeral, before she begs to re-live a moment in her life and the Stage Manager takes her back to the morning of her twelfth birthday. I'm describing the quality of presence I want the actors to have who are playing the already-dead characters—how they should sit, where their point of focus should be—when I realize they are no longer listening to me. They are looking at something over my head. I turn around, and perched on a tree branch above me, there is a medium-sized brown and white raptor. It might be a red tailed hawk, or a red shouldered hawk, but whatever it is, it is holding the back half of a rabbit in its talons, neatly split down the middle as if it recently divided the rabbit equitably with a friend who prefers the front.

The hawk looks at the actors. The actors look at the hawk. I look back and forth between them. Everyone is still. I'm sure a few people take out cameras and snap pictures, or make rabbit jokes, but the feeling of it is stillness. It is as if we were performing an idea and then the idea itself showed up. The hawk eats some of the rabbit. It seems like it will take a long time to eat it all. I don't worry about losing the last hour of rehearsal time before the sun sets. In the stillness, I can feel the echo of Wilder's words, the presence of death and of hunger, the movement of sun and shadow. Harriet Jacobs's final resting place on Clethra Path is a few minutes walk from here. I visited her and Louisa before our rehearsal today.

I can feel that I am now living the lesson it felt so painful to learn: how it is necessary as a director to stay in relationship to darkness. Only by admitting its possibility ourselves can we make space for our collaborators and for our audiences to find their own admission, and for them to feel the related possibility—though not the guarantee—of light.

Eventually, perhaps tired of being watched, or tired of watching, the bird takes its half-rabbit and flies away.

We begin our rehearsal again. The actors playing the dead sit among the graves. Emily is transported to her twelfth birthday, but is quickly overwhelmed by how unaware her mother and father seem of the sublime beauty of their ordinary lives, their lack of noticing. The actress playing Emily, in a bright red wool coat, tears on her cheeks, grabs the Stage Manager by the hands, asking with perfect urgency: "Do any human beings ever realize life as they live it?—every, every minute?"

The dead do not hear her. But they are there, waiting. They sit upright, alert but not stiff, their eyes in soft focus, only half-seeing the trees above her head.

A Play With God Inside It

A man with God inside him is still
preferable to a man with only his
breakfast inside him.

— Jeanette Winterson, *Art and Lies*

Although my brother and I were the offspring of an avowed atheist and an understated agnostic, raised in a secular household, we nonetheless turned out to be vaguely religious kids—inclined to ritual, interested in prayer, in search of dogma. Because there was no framework provided on which to hang this strange inner vastness, this electric longing, we improvised. I worshiped at the altar of the theater: making paper-doll icons of the actresses I saw in plays, memorizing and reciting their lines, and creating my own elaborate productions. When I walked into a theater, my chest expanded, sometimes to the point of physical pain. I breathed in deeply. This brought on an existential throb that resonated through my whole body and took on a pale purple glow, leaving me tongue-tied and yearning. I called this feeling "*It.*"

My brother Eric actually went so far as to develop his own religion, which he called "The Crow Clan." It involved not eating duck (or, presumably, crow—although that never came up), and creating pieces of sacred art in shoeboxes. I never completely understood The Crow Clan, but I understood the need for it. Eventually, their offspring's abiding interest in religious ritual drove my parents to enroll us in Sunday school at the Plymouth Congregational Church in downtown Seattle. I was interested in the experience—I liked the imposing scale of the building with its weird, contemporary stained glass and stucco sanctuary—*and* they had a Christmas pageant! But I felt alienated by the fact that everyone else there seemed to know and believe a bunch of stuff that I didn't. Also, it made me uncomfortable to be around people who spoke casually about God, since, in our house, that word was not in circulation. As far as I can remember, my parents never even said things like "god-given right" or "godforsaken neighborhood." Thus, at Plymouth Congregational, "God" came as an enormous shock to me every time I heard it. Plus it was weird being the kids whose parents just dropped them off and drove away, while everyone else's parents filed into the sanctuary for service, wearing nice shoes and smiling at each other. Our visits to Plymouth tapered off and finally ceased.

In her poetic study of Haitian Voudoun, *Divine Horsemen: The Living Gods of Haiti*, Maya Deren writes that ritual dances can be distinguished from secular dances not by the physical choreography but, like all sacred art, by a "special ethos," the same "quality of form" that alerts the viewer that "the painting before us is a Madonna and not a woman with a shawl." Lewis Hyde writes of the distinction a reader makes between a certain kind of paperback romance novel, mass-produced through adherence to a market-derived formula, and a book that will have enduring meaning in our lives—we recognize the former as a commodity, whereas the latter is "the gift we long for, the gift that, when it comes, speaks commandingly to the soul and irresistibly moves us." It was this gift I craved, which I would recognize by its special ethos, and which I did not find at Plymouth. But I *did* find a whisper of it in books, in going out dancing, in sitting in an audience—or rather, those things stirred a desire in me, awakening a sharp longing that daily life wanted to put to sleep. This was the feeling I knew as *It*.

Eventually I started to suspect that *It* was not just the feeling of desire but also the desired feeling—that *It* was it. From there it was a short leap to deduce that *It* was also God. God could be awakened, inside me, by the gift of a beautiful experience or a beautiful work of art. I kept this conclusion to myself.

In college, I took a religious studies course. The first assignment: identify a ritual in your life and write 1000 words about why it fits this course's definition of sacred practice.

I wrote about listening to my favorite public radio program, *This American Life*, produced by WBEZ in Chicago, and hosted by Ira Glass, who I knew had gone to the same school I did, and who sounded like someone's sexily existential older brother. "Each week we choose a theme and bring you a number of different stories on that theme," Ira would say, and the hour of storytelling unspooled. I didn't have a smart phone, I'd never heard of a "podcast"; I had to turn on my little purple radio at the right time on the right day to listen. It felt like a discovery, a secret; the staggering scope of human ambition, the folly and the genius of the human mind, the stubborn loyalty of the human heart. For my religious studies class, I wrote about how this Saturday afternoon ritual made me feel connected to the human condition across time and space, gave me a sense of my place in the universe.

I shared the essay with my parents, who were really pleased with it. At the time, I thought their pleasure came from a feeling that I had finally returned to the fold, that they saw the radio-listening ritual as an essentially secular activity.

My first job out of college was working at The 52nd Street Project, a youth theater organization in Hell's Kitchen, NYC. The 52nd Street Project was one of the best-known youth arts organizations at the time; their work had won national awards, been written about in books and in the *New York Times*. My job included teaching Playmaking, the playwriting class which served as kids' introduction to The Project, and often to theater in general. The Playmaking program had been developed and refined by Project staff and artists over the years, and was now an impeccably structured 10-week journey in which I could play my part. Each class started as a motley crew of 3rd, 4th and 5th graders from Hell's Kitchen; two months later, they were a cohort of playwrights who had written, revised, and polished their work, tweaked it further while observing rehearsals, and then watched their play performed by professional actors in front of a large and enthusiastic audience. This formula worked, like a tiny, efficient appliance, to make a writer out of any child who happened to wander in the door. After Playmaking, kids could proceed on to other programs, equally well-formulated—more writing, acting onstage themselves, close collaborations with professional artists—an elegant scaffold that would take any child who stuck with it on a decade-long artistic journey from writing a ten-minute play at age nine through performing in an international tour of a Shakespeare play by their high school graduation.

The 52nd Street Project was really good at what they did. They made, and continue to make, a significant difference in the lives of hundreds of young people every year. They even created a "replication kit" that outlines their process and structure, providing an effective seed for the establishment of similar organizations around the country.

I was 21 years old when I began working there, and it was incredible. I was exposed to the programming activities of a non-profit arts organization—serving and responding to the community, recruiting and managing interns and volunteers, creating partnerships with other organizations and businesses, contributing to big and small conversations about the kids, the plays, the artists. I could see the operational and development side, too, whirring along to support the programs—I helped set up and break down our yearly benefit gala, collected work samples from my students for grants that were being written. I got to be part of all of this in a very stable, healthy organization—a cautious organization that believed in consistency, getting one thing exactly right before moving on to the next, incremental growth. There was no anxiety over payroll, there was no frantic last minute budget-slashing, there was no hand-wringing over the effectiveness of the work or the mission. There was plenty of stress—from the long hours, from the interpersonal fatigue of office politics, from the heartbreak, and sometimes terror, of the young people we served. It wasn't a *relaxing* job, but it was to some extent a predictable one.

The staff of the Project reminded me of my parents—smart, hard-working, loving but unsentimental. They had high expectations, which I tried to live up to, and a limited amount of patience for equivocation, contemplation, or doubt. The rigorous schedule and the meticulous framework kept the focus on executing the programs to a high standard of excellence—both pedagogical and artistic. There was an interest in small adjustments that could make the work even more excellent than it already was, but little space for reflection or ideation, scarce opportunity to dream into what else might be possible. We certainly never spoke directly of the sacred realm. The 52nd Street Project felt like a secular place.

But just under the surface, in moments that passed in a blink—the look on a child's face in the breath before the audience erupted in applause at the end of her play—there was holiness beyond measure, a holiness I squirreled away in my chest. When I was overwhelmed by the force of what I felt, I tried to hide it. I felt that *It* was not welcomed; our work was to serve these kids in a grounded and deeply present way. There was too much real work to be done in the real world to be carried away by the divine, the ineffable.

The 52nd Street Project was a wonderful place to work and I could probably have worked there happily for a very long time. But I was in love, so I moved back to Rhode Island to see if that could turn out the way I wanted it to (spoiler: it didn't). In Rhode Island, along with the demise of my relationship, I encountered The Providence Black Repertory Company. Black Rep had just moved into an old department store on Westminster Street in historic downtown Providence. Huge storefront windows framed an intimate lounge with deep leather armchairs, gold and red Moroccan ottomans, and carved wooden side tables, hugged by a sprawling L-shaped bar. A heavy curtain could be drawn to bisect the space, separating the bar and lounge area—called "The Xxodus Café"—from the back half of the room, where our theater performances took place. The idiosyncratic layout put the stage in one corner, surrounded on two sides with an intricate vinyl tiled floor, cushy red booths, and cabaret tables. After theater performances, we'd open the curtain and lift turntables onto the stage, and the whole thing would transform into a venue for live music and dancing. If you happened to be working late in the offices upstairs, the walls would shake with bass.

I became the Associate Director, in charge of all of the theater programming. In addition to the theater season, there were nightly live music performances, a summer arts festival, and a full slate of education programs in local schools. Unlike The 52nd Street Project in almost every way, Black Rep was a young organization growing in leaps and bounds, constantly re-inventing programming and trying new things, a daily diet of risk and experiment. When I expressed nervousness about whether we had the money or expertise or space or goodwill to do something, the founding artistic director, Donald W. King, repeated this refrain: "Anxiety blocks your creativity." Donald was equal parts intellectual and mystic. We read a lot of Rumi.

> *Don't open the door to the study and begin reading.*
> *Take down a musical instrument.*
> *Let the beauty we love be what we do.*
> *There are hundreds of ways to kneel and kiss the ground.*

I read tons of plays. I created budgets for a theater season. I researched and wrote grants, I met with the graphic designer to develop concepts and oversee timelines for marketing collateral, I set ticket prices, wrote press releases, hired and fired box office staff, organized auditions, negotiated with the actor's union, and, often, worked late into the night so I could keep an ear on the rehearsals happening outside my office. I tried to get reviewers to come to the show, planned the opening night party, gave notes to the director, made sure performances were ending in time for the actors to catch their trains home, gave the curtain speech, led talkbacks on Sundays, and often—what the hell—put on a little lip gloss and stayed for the dancing.

In *Utopia in Performance*, Jill Dolan speaks of some performances as messianic in the "Benjaminian" sense, per Walter Benjamin who believed that "one of the foremost tasks of art has always been the creation of a demand which could be fully satisfied only later." These messianic performances reach towards an imagined future moment of transformation (or, for Benjamin, revolution), "images toward which, without knowing their real contours, without the necessity that they be fixed or real, we direct our hope." This feeling permeated everything we did at Black Rep. There was a constant sense of motion towards a shimmering, critical, yet unknown future, an anticipatory urgency. Every decision—season selection, hiring, the image on the front of the postcard—was spiked with this kind of "reaching towards."

We talked about the invisible, the transformative, in the same breath as the budget. I remember sitting at my dining table with Donald until 3 a.m. crafting a set of Core Artistic Values, finishing a draft at the same time we finished a bottle of Diplomatico Reserva rum. I also remember the series of brown-bag lunch talks we had for staff discussing the meaning of "diaspora," the summer music festival where we danced all night in the middle of Westminster Street, the elders who would come up to me after a matinee, crying, and clasp both of my hands in theirs. I remember kneeling by the side of the Providence River at dawn dressed all in white, leaving an offering of fresh fruit to bless our artistic endeavors.

Unlike my job at The 52nd Street Project, literally *nothing* at Black Rep was fixed in place. Sometimes this was enraging, like going to work every day on an ocean liner, and every time you start to get something done, there's a big wave and all the furniture slides across the cabin and as you're chasing after the desk, you're thinking "*Why can't we just nail it to floor?*" But more often than not, it was exciting. We experimented with everything—the ideal curtain time, how to print tickets, whether or not to have subscriptions, partnerships with other organizations. Once we had a guy cooking and serving up several flavors of crickets in the lobby pre-show. Most of our experiments related, not to the productions themselves, but to the context in which they were presented. As an audience member, we reasoned, what you know about the mission of the theater, the way the poster looks, what you've seen about the play on social media—all these shape your expectations before you even reach the door of the theater. Once there, you absorb the energy of the lobby and your interactions with folks working the box office and concessions. The pre-show music and curtain speech are your direct point of entry into the performance. While many theaters might think of these as a combination of marketing and customer service concerns—making sure the poster is alluring and the curtain speech sells subscriptions (marketing), making sure the tickets are ready, the drinks are cold, and the staff is welcoming (customer service)—at Black Rep, we thought of these as opportunities to make an invitation to an audience. And it's the invitation, the invocation, that opens the channel to divinity.

We knew we had to print a program for each show—crediting artists and printing ads from our sponsors—but we wondered about how to maximize the impact of this significant expense. Our answer was *Black Notes*, a "program 'zine" which included traditional playbill components like actor bios, alongside poetry, interviews, images, quotes, and scholarly articles. We built each season of *Black Notes* around a theme (one year it was "Promised Land," the next "Skeletons in the Closet") which was reflected in the plays in the theater season, the carnival parade in Black Rep's summer music festival, and educational workshops. Because it didn't look or feel like a playbill, and because the building was a bar and music venue when it wasn't a theater, the content got into much wider circulation. Patrons read it while they had a drink at the bar, teaching artists brought it into schools with them—and, I imagined, someone who had never been to Black Rep might pick up her daughter's copy of *Black Notes* off the kitchen table at home.

We thought audience "talkbacks" were important, but we wanted to avoid two things: free-wheeling discussions dominated by a few loud voices, and conversations that allowed artists to hold forth on artistic process rather than engaging in a meaningful dialogue about the play's content. We hoped for less of a traditional "talkback" and more of a "talk-back-and-forth"—where hard questions could be raised and divergent opinions could be discussed with curiosity and respect. We tried and rejected a few formats before settling on a modified version of Liz Lerman's Critical Response Process. First, the audience would be asked to share brief affirmations—what did you see that you liked, that impacted you, that moved you? The second step was to posit a question—a real question, one that we'd struggled with during the rehearsal process—for audience discussion. Finally, audience members were invited to ask their own questions of us or each other. The three-part structure, along with strong facilitation, gave us a clear container and discouraged rambling, discursive comments.

The audience was game for this kind of conversation, but for it to work, we realized we had to train the artists, too. The artists onstage had to actually believe that we were not experts, that the audience had something new to teach us about a play we'd been immersed in for weeks. I remember the revelation I had, leading talkbacks for the final show I directed at Black Rep, that the dynamic of the talkback was reflecting back my own rehearsal dynamic to me. If I had modeled a generous co-creation of knowledge and an openness to other perspectives in rehearsal, the actors would do the same with the audience in the talkback, often even echoing language I'd used in the rehearsal room.

Our experiments at Black Rep—with playbills and talkbacks and many other things—were both imaginative and practical. Black Rep was comfortable with being both a Madonna and a woman with a shawl; I think we imagined it as a kind of crossroads where the Madonna and the shawl-wearing woman could drink a few shots of Diplomatico together and argue about colonialism.

The crossroads, in Haitian voudoun, is the most fertile and also the most volatile place. Deren writes that many drawings and paintings used in voudoun ritual present a vertical axis intersecting a horizontal one. In these sacred images, called *vever* in Kreyol, the horizontal axis is the material world, as we see it in our daily lives. The vertical plane is the spiritual dimension, the unseen world. The intersection of the two represents the point of contact, the place where that which is beyond this world is reflected *in* the world, the site of "what could and should be… the metaphysical processional."

When I first saw these images, I thought that in a theatrical sense the horizontal axis could represent plays concerned with the life of the body, the family, the intellect, the social system—naturalistic "living room" plays, social dramas, history and biography plays. The vertical axis would be for plays concerned with the invisible world, the life of the spirit and the unconscious—dream plays, poetic plays, lyrical plays, plays that felt less terrestrial and more celestial. The horizontal axis would be Miller, Shaw, Lorraine Hansberry, Emily Mann. The vertical axis might include August Strindberg, Adrienne Kennedy, Chuck Mee. Then there are those who travel intentionally on both axes: Maria Irene Fornes, Sam Shepard, August Wilson.

But the text alone does not determine our view of whether, to paraphrase Jeanette Winterson, a play has some God in it, or only its breakfast. It is all too frequently possible to be transported by one encounter with a work of art, only to find yourself unmoved by the same play in a different production, or even the same production on a different day—like returning to a restaurant hoping for a repeat of the sublime first meal you ate there, only to be disappointed.

Why do we experience some encounters with works of art as holy, and others, seemingly equally compelling and well-crafted, as interesting but secular? Some of it has to do with those elements of invitation—the temperature of the room, the tone of the curtain speech. Much of it has to do with the text of the play, and with the choices that have been made during the creative process, the production's aesthetic. And some of it, I'm sure, has nothing to do with the work of art at all, and more to do with the state of our minds and hearts at the moment of the encounter. But perhaps a *receptive* audience encountering a *beautifully attuned* work of art in a *thoughtfully structured* context can add up in a sort of alchemical mathematics, like the Haitian equations Deren writes about:

> *In Voudoun one* and *one make three; two* and *two make five; for the* and *of the equation is the third and fifth part, respectively, the relationship which makes all the parts meaningful... The figure five is as the four of the cross-roads plus the swinging of the door which is the point itself of crossing, the moment of arrival and departure.*

The "*and*" is the relationship of the parts to one another that makes all the parts meaningful, and, sometimes, makes it all add up to more than it should.

The text of the play is one part. The aesthetic of the production is another part. The context surrounding the event, yet another. And then there is the *And* of the relationship between the parts, the swinging door. The whole picture, like the *vever*, must allow space for convergence, a pause at the crossroads, an opening through which what could be, what should be, might enter. This is the gift I long for. Such a performance—inviting, questioning, reaching towards—feels, to me, like a play with God inside it. I remember the tongue-tied yearning I felt in the theater as a child, the pulsing purple light, the throb of *It* in my ribcage. I thought *It* was my longing for God. Then I thought perhaps *It* <u>was</u> God. Now I wonder if I was looking for the space for God to enter. *It* was that space—and the feeling of that space inside me being made—the glow that gave me access to everything sacred around me.

I sometimes felt so alone with my family; the most vivid thing in my experience was a thing that they didn't believe in. If I am unaccountably moved by something, if it fills me and changes me, and you tell me that thing doesn't exist, then how can we be looking at the same thing, in the same space? Is it possible for it to be a sacred mystery to me, and simply a pleasant evening to you? Working at Black Rep helped me understand that it could all exist together, the sacred and the profane, the scientist and the artist.

So now I believe in leaving a little bit of room. It might mean holding a few extra beats in the final blackout before the curtain call music plays; it could be allowing the dinner break to go longer than scheduled because the laughter is sparkling, filling the rehearsal hall; sometimes it means reading the scene again without analyzing it, without questioning it. It means giving artists enough room to feel their own instincts, resting for a moment instead of rushing forward, breathing into discomfort and into beauty. It means leaving a little bit of doubt, a little bit of silence, a pause at the crossroads—a space for God to enter.

In 2009, Black Rep closed its doors permanently. In an all too familiar story for small arts nonprofits, the organization grew quickly, energized by rapturous community response to its slate of ambitious programing, yet expenses and debt swiftly overtook resources and support.

I recently did an interview with a student who was going through some of the Black Rep's archival materials for a project. The interview was videotaped and is now posted online. Towards the end of the interview, he asks me "What do you think Black Rep left behind, in terms of its legacy?" I immediately start listing the artists who worked with us as teenagers who are now performing off-Broadway, writing for television, and leading organizations. It impacted a generation of artists, I say, an outsized impact given the size of the organization and its relatively brief existence. Then I sigh and look down, running my hand through my hair. "There are so many more Black arts organizations that have folded than are still standing," I say, leaning forward, "And to some extent, I see the legacy of Black Rep as part of a tragic legacy of other Black arts organizations, arts organizations of color, queer arts organizations, that are providing something really vital and yet are living on the razor's edge of existence in a society that isn't particularly invested in lifting up the stories of those communities. Black Rep made a huge impact on a lot of people. And it broke a lot of people's hearts."

One of those heartbroken young artists was Natalie Marshall Hirsch, still in college when Black Rep closed, who went on to get a graduate degree in Arts Education from NYU. When my old job at The 52nd Street Project, Associate Artistic Director, became available, I encouraged her to apply. She got the job, she excelled, and a few years later, she became the Artistic Director of that organization. I like to think that she's carried a little bit of the DNA of Black Rep into The 52nd Street Project. Maybe it's my imagination, but when I go back to visit, it feels more spacious to me now.

But this is a book about endings, after all. The end of a theater is different from the end of a play. The end of Black Rep swung back to bowl me over with a force equal to everything I'd poured into it, all the long nights and early mornings, all of the dreams and the reaching towards, all the learning and the stretching, snapping back like a giant rubber band to use the force of my own love against me. The loss was visceral, tactile—I missed the *place*, the incense-and-rum smell of it, the heaviness of the red velvet curtains, the stickiness of the bar under my hand, the vibration of the bass through the floor, the height of the room from the mezzanine as I leaned over to see the audience settling in for the second act—and it hurt my spirit. I'd believed in this with more force than I'd ever believed in anything. I tried to re-orient myself to my career, my sense of purpose. What could I do, now, going forward? I found myself disoriented, for years.

I remember reading once that however long you've been in a relationship with someone, it will take you about half that time to be fully "over" them. By this logic, having worked at Black Rep for five years, it should have taken me two and a half years to recover from losing it. I'm not sure if that arithmetic is accurate or not. I did try to move on—working for another theater, with another mission, in another city. But it was never the same. I transitioned into a freelance career, not tied to any one theater, but making work all over the country. Sometime later, I found myself building a solo performance in collaboration with a wonderful artist who lived in Providence, and they had the opportunity to perform the piece in the former Black Rep space.

So, with my new collaborator, I stepped back in the building for the first time since it had been mine. Black Rep had been gone for several years, and another performance venue was using the former Xxodus Cafe space downstairs, but apparently the second floor, where we'd had our offices, remained unused. Someone told me that the building was being cleaned out soon and said I should look around upstairs to see if there was anything I wanted.

I climbed the old wooden stairs, remembering that when we built them they were supposed to be temporary; we planned to put in an elevator. Upstairs, I wandered around in a daze, not really knowing what to do. I remember my mind fastened on a beautiful boxed set of August Wilson's plays that had been gifted to us by an artist; I thought, I should find those books, I should have them. I opened the old doors. There were our files, our posters, our photos. There was my office, looking for all the world like I'd just stepped out—but it wasn't like walking back into a Technicolor memory, it was more like walking through Pompeii. It was the same place, but covered in dust and ash, holding the vacated shapes of those who'd had to flee or who'd been buried here. I was only able to stay up there for perhaps ten minutes; I quickly staggered back down the stairs, carrying with me just one thing—not the Wilson books, which I never found, but a small blue suitcase, painted by a local graffiti artist to look like the sky on a sunny day, that had been a central element of one of my favorite productions, the world premiere of Zakiyyah Alexander's *The Etymology of Bird*. I thought—this suitcase represents everything I take with me, that I'll always carry with me, from this place.

I put the suitcase in the back seat of my car, where it stayed overnight because I was too tired to bring it inside when I got home to Boston very late that night. The next morning, my car, parked at the end of my block, was caught in a freak flash flood. Water filled the vehicle, almost lifting it off the ground. After the water receded, a tow truck came and towed away the car and everything in it.

A part of me still feels that little suitcase, painted like heaven, was responsible for the flood. *Let it go*, said the universe, the elements, the divine processional. *It's over now.*

———

I once heard Ira Glass say in an interview that he doesn't believe in anything. I'm fairly certain he shares my parents' views on God. And yet, I've been listening to *This American Life* for almost twenty-five years now, and I can recognize that it has more than just its breakfast inside it. From the beginning, it has lived and breathed at the crosswords, assembling its pieces with an *and* that lifts the whole above the sum of its parts.

My parents loved that essay I wrote for my sophomore religious studies class about *This American Life* as sacred ritual. At the time, I thought it was because they approved of my approach—intellectual, secular, reasonable—and congratulated themselves on how well I'd turned out without God. But now, it seems more likely to me that they were pleased by the essay because I'd found a way to translate the ache inside me into words, set down in an order that said something true about me, that allowed them a glimpse inside the mystery of my mind. I'm not a parent, yet, but I can imagine that the longing to understand your child's brain, to see the contents of their heart, is a more potent longing than any I have yet experienced.

When my parents come to see plays I direct, if I can, I like to sit in a place in the theater where I can watch their faces. Mostly it's to see if they like it or they hate it. Are they laughing? Often they are. Are they sleeping? Yes, sometimes. Do they, maybe, see me a little bit more clearly, every time?

Up until I was eight years old, we lived in Seattle's Fremont neighborhood; the drive home took us down a hill with a panoramic view of the mountains (at least, when the mountains were "out," as they say in Seattle—as if the mountains are a dog that someone lets in and out on some maddeningly irregular schedule). One night, driving home, my father slowed the car at the top of the hill, so that we could admire the extraordinary sunset unfolding over the mountains, a flaming riot of pink and orange. My mother, my father, my infant brother, and I stared out the window, our faces bathed in a rosy glow. There was a long silence. I thought, "This is an important moment in your life because it is Beautiful and you are Here. Pay attention. Take a picture of this in your mind and never forget it." I never have.

As a child, I imagined myself isolated in this experience—that I alone recognized the holiness of the moment, that it was precious, in that particularly sacred way, only to me. I had not yet learned how many hundreds of ways there are to kneel and kiss the ground. It was, after all, my mother who exclaimed over the sunset, my father who slowed the car, Eric who did not fuss; I leaned forward, breathing into the silence. The invisible *And* vibrated. Even in a car half-full of skeptics, it had that special ethos, that quality of form; at the top of that hill in Fremont, there we were at the crossroads—inside the metaphysical processional, ushered into the divine hush of communion.

Unstable Ground

When I was in fifth grade at Madrona Elementary School in Seattle, I was one of a small group of students pulled out of class each week to work with two professional theater artists. I remember the thrill of walking through the empty hallways while everyone else was in class to meet the rest of the group in the cafeteria. We were given writing prompts—about our school, our friends, our dreams and our fears—and we handed in our responses on slips of brownish loose-leaf paper, the kind that would rip if you erased too hard.

In those writing sessions, I sat next to kids I'd never talked to before, although we were in the same grade in the same school. This was because I was "IPP" and they were "Regular." I understood this to mean that I'd passed a test to be in a special classroom and they hadn't, and also that I had to ride the bus across town to get to Madrona, but they lived nearby and might even be able to walk to school.

An official history of the Seattle Public Schools explains that "as part of the desegregation plan's magnet program, in 1978 Madrona was made home of an elementary program for highly capable students, known as the Individualized Progress Program or IPP." It goes on to outline that IPP students came by bus from all over the city and shared the building with students in the regular elementary program, and that originally, the two groups had music, art, and physical education classes together, before eventually being "completely separated." The document also mentions that in the late 80's, IPP was renamed the Accelerated Progress Program, or APP. It does not mention whether the program's re-naming was in response to the "I pee-pee!" jokes students endured on the playground. It also doesn't mention that the arrangement at Madrona, made in the name of desegregation, essentially created a segregated student body—the "Regular" classrooms were mostly Black kids and the "IPP" classrooms were mostly not.

I'd never been told I was white, or told that I wasn't. I knew I was Armenian and Jewish. But it was clear to me at Madrona that, in a Black and white world, I was a white kid. Since the Black kids were in different classes, they sat at different lunch tables; since they lived in different neighborhoods, they went home on different buses. The theater artists who came to visit in fifth grade had selected half their cast from our IPP class, and half from the Regular classes. They went away for a few weeks and came back with a play made up entirely of our words. There were even songs, the lyrics assembled from what we'd written carefully on those slips of brown paper.

In the play, our school was "a happy place, like a rainbow"— but with a deep-running rift down the middle, "like the San Andreas fault." Six months later, when the Quake of '89 hit the

Bay Area, I thought immediately of this lyric. The performance ended with us all joining hands and singing, "Stop playing this game, we are all the same, we are all the same." We'd written the lyrics; we knew it was what we were supposed to write, both dramaturgically and morally. But, in spite of the pleasure of singing it in the cafeteria to a packed crowd, we never did figure out how to share a lunch table with our castmates. Afterwards, life continued in its usual segregated fashion at Madrona Elementary. I don't remember becoming friends with anyone in the cast. I don't even remember my castmates' names or their faces. I do remember that after the play I was more aware of our lunch-time segregation. I was able to look across the room and see the kids I was not sitting with. I don't remember how, or if, I tried to make sense of it. What I do remember, with utter clarity, is the song, which I can sing to this day. It echoes cheerily in my head: we are all the same, we are all the same.

One of my first jobs as a freelance theater artist took me back to Seattle, where I worked with a student in a BFA acting program—let's call him Alejandro—who identified as "a proud Chicano." I asked him about his experience being a student of color in a predominately white college. "Oh no," he said immediately, "I don't bring *that* into the room there." What about when he played Othello, I asked? What was the race of the character? "Um, I guess he was Black. We never really talked about it," he said. In fact, he offered with a sigh, there was only one time that his race had been referenced by a director or teacher: in the chorus of a musical, he'd been asked to bring some of his "Latin machismo" to the reading of his one line of dialogue. Alejandro told me that once he finished school he planned to pursue a career in solo performance. The only way he could conceive of to bring his whole self into the room was to build the room himself.

This was early 2009, the height of the American post-racial fantasy, the national equivalent of joining hands and singing, "We are all the same!" Alejandro, like many students of color I talked to in BFA and MFA programs, wasn't able to find the words, or the energy, to speak to the harm of this narrative—to explain to his teachers that to tell him he was "the same" was to erase him, and the uniqueness of his experience. That the impulse, however politically correct, not to discuss his race in relationship to the characters he played was to tacitly request that he play them, and that they function within the world of the play, as culturally normative, a.k.a. white (with the confusing exception of Othello). Anne Bogart writes that, "an actor senses the quality of the [director's] watching… the one gift we can give to another human being is our attention." As cared for as he felt on many other levels by his directors and teachers, Alejandro sensed that the quality of their watching was incomplete.

A few months later, my father and I went to see the Broadway revival of *Joe Turner's Come and Gone*, produced by Lincoln

Center Theater (LCT). I was excited to see it because it was both of our favorite of August Wilson's plays, and because the theater community was abuzz over the fact that it was directed by Bartlett Sher, then the Artistic Director of Intiman Theatre (in Seattle) and A White Guy. Although the whiteness of a director of a Broadway show doesn't usually make headlines, this time it did, since during his lifetime Wilson had famously refused to allow white directors for major productions of his work. In his 1997 address to Theater Communications Group, "The Ground on Which I Stand," Wilson advocated for a Black Theater, declaring that he was from the tradition of Black artists that performed in the slave quarters for other Blacks, and not in the big house for whites. Although his views were decried by some as separatist, Wilson stood his ground during his lifetime. After his death, his widow, Constanza Romero, was faced with the task of honoring his views while allowing his work to take its rightful, expansive place in the American cannon. She chose to green-light Sher as director for *Joe Turner*'s return to Broadway.

August Wilson and I lived in Seattle almost exactly the same amount of time—me for the first sixteen years of my life, and he for the last fifteen years of his. When my immigrant great-grandparents arrived in this country, they settled in Eastern cities—Boston, Philadelphia—and all of us are still here, more or less along the Atlantic. The Seattle years were a brief Western interlude in the life of my family, but they were critical years for me, and for Wilson too—seeing the premieres of five of the ten plays of his American Century Cycle, as well as his autobiographical solo performance *How I Learned What I Learned* and the iconic "Ground" speech.

Wilson didn't write the Century Cycle in chronological order. The last two plays he wrote were the beginning of the cycle—*Gem of the Ocean*, set in 1904—and its ending—*Radio Golf*, set in 1997. As a director, this order makes sense to me—the beginning and the end are always the last pieces to fall into place. *Gem* reached Broadway in 2004 while *Radio Golf* had its regional premiere just months before Wilson's death in 2005.

My parents took me and my brother to see that Broadway production of *Gem of The Ocean*, starring Phylicia Rashad and Ruben Santiago-Hudson, directed by Kenny Leon—it was Christmastime, and very cold. I was completely overwhelmed; I remember stepping out onto the frigid street afterwards still weeping and feeling self-conscious because I couldn't explain why. *Gem* immediately became my second favorite Wilson play—behind *Joe Turner*, the fourth play he wrote and the second in the cycle, taking place in 1911. Maybe I loved it partly because I knew it was my dad's favorite, but I think we were both drawn to the ritual and magic in it, and to its sense of optimism and possibility. Unlike the plays on either side of it—*Gem* and *Ma Rainey's Black Bottom*, set in 1927—the play does not end with the violent death of one Black man at the hands of another. Rather, it ends with a transcendent mutual salvation.

The play begins in a Pittsburgh boardinghouse on the day a mysterious stranger, Herald Loomis, arrives with his young daughter Zonia. They are seeking Loomis' wife, Zonia's mother, Martha. Loomis explains that he was snatched by Joe Turner when Zonia was just an infant, bound into labor for seven years, before being released as mysteriously as he'd been taken. But when he returned, his wife was gone. He is determined to find her so he can begin fresh.

Bynum, another boarder at the house, is one of Wilson's great griot characters; born into slavery, he now earns his living as a rootworker, practicing folk medicine with a specialty in "binding people together." Early in the play, Bynum recalls a long ago meeting with a "shiny man" who showed him the secret of life, a man who "had this light coming out of him… he shining like new money with that light." The shiny man ushers Bynum to a dream place where he connects with his ancestors and discovers his personal song, the Binding Song. Bynum longs to see another shiny man before he dies, so that "I would know that my song had been accepted and worked its full power in the world and that I could lay down and die a happy man."

Bynum quickly recognizes Loomis as a person who's been separated from his own song. At the end of the first act, as the group engages in an after-dinner juba—a celebratory call and response dance—Loomis is plunged into a nightmarish recall. He describes a vision of people made of bones rising up from the ocean—which would later, or earlier, depending on which chronology you use, be conjured by Aunt Ester in *Gem of the Ocean*—and feeling himself among them, washed onto shore. But as the others get up and begin to walk down the road, he is unable to move. "The ground's starting to shake," he cries, "The world's busting half in two… my legs won't stand up!" The first act ends with Loomis collapsed on the floor.

By the end of the second act, Loomis does find his wife Martha—a reunion that quickly builds to a tense standoff as Loomis suspects that Bynum's binding spell was responsible for his years of wandering. Loomis pulls out a knife, lashing out against the forces that have bound him—Bynum, Joe Turner, the church. Finally Loomis slashes himself across the chest with his knife and rubs the blood over his face. Suddenly, he is struck with a revelation. "I'm standing!," he cries, "I'm standing. My legs stood up! I'm standing now!"

Having found his song, Wilson's stage direction tells us, Loomis is resurrected, cleansed, given breath and is now free to soar. As he runs out of the boardinghouse, the play's final line belongs to Bynum, who cries, 'Herald Loomis, you shining! You shining like new money!"

I'd only ever read the play and, in spite of the furor over Sher, was incredibly excited to see it. It began beautifully—with Loomis, holding Zonia by the hand, walking the road against a massive sunrise. The cast was fantastic, bringing Wilson's text into poetic, nimble, funny, wonderful life. The scenic design had minimal pieces of furniture floating surreally on and off stage in front of gorgeous fields of saturated color—which was pretty if somewhat overly tidy. In fact, the overall feel of the production was a bit sterile ("well-scrubbed," as an online reader of the *Times* review commented). For example, at one point the actors gently carried live doves across the stage, a rather precious move in a play whose opening scene includes a detailed narration of a ritual pigeon-sacrifice. Though the text describes the slitting of throats, the pouring of blood, the burial in the ground, that sense of dirt and blood and ritual was notably absent from this production.

I remember feeling, at intermission, pleased to be seeing the play and underwhelmed by the production. And that might have been how I felt after the curtain, too, if the production hadn't concluded with a design choice I will never forget. As Loomis rubbed blood across his chest, gold glitter showered down across the stage. As Bynum cried his final line "You shining like new money!", he stretched his arms out to glory in the glitter like a summer rain. At the moment when I should have been left breathless in my seat, too overwhelmed even to applaud, I turned to my dad and whispered, "Was that... glitter?"

To my eye, so much of the complex power of Wilson's perfect ending was made illegible by that veil of gold glitter. The shiny man in Wilson's text is a metaphor, of course, but in this production the metaphorical shine was undercut by the presence of literal shine, which stripped the poetry of its power, making it one thing instead of many. In Wilson's ending, there is violence and love, blood and light, the pain of the past and the tragic promise of a future we know from a historical perspective will be both more wonderful and more terrible than anything these characters could have imagined. In Sher's ending, the totalizing shower of gold glitter insisted on a harmonization of these complex tensions—literally filling the space of the story, covering everything. In Wilson's happy ending the pain of the past is allowed to be present, can be metabolized and carried forward into a hope for the future all the more extraordinary for what has been risked to attain it. In Sher's happy ending, a veil of radiance wipes away everything that has come before it while also obscuring the subsequent years of violence just over the horizon.

When I got home, I googled the creative team for the production. Acclaimed African-American artists Taj Mahal and Dianne McIntyre created the transition music and juba staging, respectively, but the production's visual designs were created by a team of seasoned Lincoln Center designers and Sher collaborators who appear, from their photographs, to be white. Of course, as a director, you want a team that shares your aesthetic and understands your vision; I, like Sher, try to engage designers with whom I already have strong working relationships and a shared vocabulary. But decisions about sets and lights are not only about the way things look; a production's aesthetic isn't just cosmetic, it also establishes point of view. I had the nagging feeling that what *Variety* called the "shimmering beauty" of

Sher's production was the totalizing effect of a mostly-white creative team's point of view. It felt akin to a Broadway-sized chorus of "we are all the same."

In a blog on the LCT website, Sher introduced his concept for the scenic design by describing how Wilson's longtime collaborator Lloyd Richards, who directed *Joe Turner*'s premiere on Broadway in 1988, worked in a tradition of "deep naturalism"; in contrast, Sher and his set designer were "more attracted by the poet in August Wilson." The costume design, too, leaned away from realism into a sense of airiness, "looking more like 1912 than 1911... less Victorian, less buttoned-up." The overall effect, Sher said, would be to evoke "a sense that a seismic shift is taking place in the country. In 1911, as in our own day, people have a sense that five years from now things will be very different than how they are today."

What was the transformative moment Sher was theorizing for Wilson's 1911 characters? The publicity materials for the production emphasized that the play was set at the beginning of the Great Migration, the movement of 6 million African Americans from the South toward the industrial cities of the North. Though the dates don't precisely line up—most sources put the beginning stirrings of the Great Migration at 1915 or 1916—the play does have an energy of movement and opportunity that supports this reading. So the production concept seems to have sprung from an explicit comparison between the Great Migration and the election of Obama, theorizing both moments as transformative for African Americans. The decision to move away from "deep naturalism" and towards "poetry" was intended to give us the sense of anticipation of this seismic shift.

Although a major geographic change was on its way in 1911, it seems premature to announce that a "seismic shift" would occur in the experience of Black Americans in the years subsequent to Joe Turner's exit. The following decade saw the height of Jim Crow and the rise of the KKK. The move Northwards, while opening up opportunities, also revealed new systems of bias and new kinds of violence. Nothing demonstrates this better than Wilson's plays themselves. The next play in the cycle, *Ma Rainey's Black Bottom*, is one of the most tragic. Set in Chicago in 1927, it's also the only play that doesn't take place in Pittsburgh, giving us a clear snapshot of what life was like for those who were part of the Northward tide of the Great Migration.

Sher's pristine embrace of the poetic elided the complexity of these realities—the ones we could know (what would follow the Great Migration), and the ones we couldn't (what would follow the election of Obama). This is not to deny the poetry in *Joe Turner* or any of Wilson's work. The play is at once lyrical and familiar, sweeping and intimate. Past and present collide, as do the realms of visible and invisible. A production that emphasized only the "deep naturalism" at the expense of the "shimmering beauty" would certainly miss the point, and vice versa. But it is not just the presence of naturalistic and poetic elements that matters in *Joe Turner*. The play's beating heart lies in the *tension* between epic and ordinary. This tension is an aesthetic reminder of the collision of grief and praise—the wrenching heart of the blues—that characterizes Wilson's confrontation with American history. His characters live with this tension; his audiences should too. The pain of history is ever-present—and at the end, made visible in the blood on Loomis' face. It is this pain which both haunts and cleanses Loomis. To glitterize the moment is to upset this fragile balance—a disservice to Wilson's complex, transcendent finale.

"I've learned more from this cast than any group that I've ever worked with," Sher said in a *New York Times* article. "But I also learned an enormous amount about the lack of opportunity in theater today. More Ibsen should be directed by Black directors. More Shakespeare. More Chekhov." In a later radio interview, Sher said he felt a sense of responsibility to make such hires at his own theater and "that's what every theater needs to be doing, so that everybody's expanding equally. I think that's the transition we're in now. Whereas those rules are going to start to dissolve and separate, and we're going to have less ability to look, in the next generation of directors, at such clear boundaries about who does what work… It's a step along the way to making sure that people think in less prescribed categories about who they hire for what kinds of shows."

The past decade has not borne out Sher's prophecy. Sher himself stepped down from Intiman shortly after directing *Joe Turner*, so we'll never know if he would have made these changes at his own theater. What we do know is that there has not been a boom in Black directors doing Ibsen and Chekhov; I struggle to think of even one instance of this in a high-profile professional setting. August Wilson has twice since come to Broadway, both times directed by Black men (*Fences*, directed by Kenny Leon in 2010, and *Jitney*, directed by Ruben Santiago-Hudson in 2017); however, the overall picture of who is directing on Broadway has not shifted. There are no official published statistics on the demographics of Broadway directors, but in my own count of the 2018 Broadway season, 3 of the 38 productions listed no director, and of the remaining 35, 32 had white directors. Only two directors of color were represented, both of them African American men, one of whom (again, Leon) directed two productions. Only four shows were directed by women. And in 2018, no female directors of color were represented on Broadway. Bart Sher, incidentally, had two shows on Broadway that year.

"Culture is one part of what's at play," Sher explained in that radio interview, "but there's a lot of other things which make good storytelling work… That's my job that I bring to it. That's my skill." Bart Sher is a perceptive and exacting director, known for extensive research and rigorous craft. He must have believed that his particular artistic perspective could illuminate new and interesting facets of Wilson's work, revealing a *Joe Turner* for the Obama era. But by placing "culture" and "skill" as separate facets of the qualifications necessary to direct August Wilson, he contradicts Wilson's own insistence that his work, though shaped by aesthetic influences from Aristotle to Shaw, was necessarily and primarily grounded in the specifics of Black life and African American history. For Wilson, culture and skill could not be separated. And though Wilson himself often said that the human themes of his work were universal, he was also clear that the specific experiences used to convey those themes were not universal. In "Ground," he reiterates that he and his work stand "squarely on the self-defining ground of the slave quarters," the "high ground of self-definition" that is derived from the experience, history, and spiritual knowledge of African-Americans. Regardless of the race of the director, I don't think it is possible to successfully direct Wilson's work without a foundation on this ground.

Although the choice of Sher to direct *Joe Turner* on Broadway generated much public and private debate, the reception of the production itself was generally positive. The critical reception was enthusiastic, verging on rapturous. There were Tony nominations (and a win for actor Roger Robinson); the *Times* second-string critic, Charles Isherwood, wrote his own piece on the production after it had already been reviewed by Ben Brantley, revealing that he had seen the show twice and was "willing to wander Times Square wearing a sandwich board to spread the gospel of its glory." A good number of critics agreed with Isherwood that production was a marked improvement on the "deep naturalism" approach, allowing Wilson's poetry to find its true form. Then again, out of the dozens of reviews,

I couldn't find one that was written by a non-white reviewer. It is exhausting reading review after review making sweeping statements about how beautiful Sher has made Wilson's play— as per the *Lighting and Sound America* rave declaring that "in Sher's hands, *Joe Turner's Come and Gone* is finally fulfilled as both a comic drama of Black life in the early 20th century and as an incantatory vision of the Black race at a turning point."

Who gets to decide when a play is "finally fulfilled"? That would be a rhetorical question, except, as things stood in 2009, and as they still stand today, it's not. The critics—mostly white, mostly male, mostly of a certain age—get to say. Who gets to direct (and design and produce) plays on Broadway, or at Lincoln Center? Again, the unfortunate answer is all too obvious. In fact, it turns out that at the time Sher's *Joe Turner* arrived on Broadway, a non-white director hadn't helmed a Lincoln Center Theater production in eighteen years. *Eighteen years!* This piece of information was not reported in any of the articles surrounding the furor over Sher's selection as director, but emerged in an investigative segment some months later on public radio's *Studio 360*. In a follow-up segment, Lincoln Center Artistic Director Andre Bishop said he had learned a lot from the experience, and was in the process of meeting with every Black director that contacted him. He predicted that in two or three years, LCT's track record would look very different. "We haven't hired any African Americans in a long long time, as you said. And I feel that was a terrible mistake, and I'm changing it... I have nothing defensive to say about this, because I feel I have not behaved as thoughtfully as I might have."

———

A few years after Sher's *Joe Turner*, I applied and was admitted to the Lincoln Center Theater Director's Lab—a developmental summer program for directors from around the world. I was part of a cohort of 70 directors ranging wildly in age, nationality, and aesthetic. Between sessions, we ate our bag lunches next to the marble fountains, and got lost in the labyrinthine corridors of the LCT basement. It was thrilling and agitating and disorienting. In the second week, I saw on the schedule that Andre Bishop was coming down for an hour-long Q&A with us. I wrote out a question in my spiral notebook, and, partway into the session, nervously raised my hand. I spoke to the power of being there at Lincoln Center and thanked Bishop for speaking with us. I then recalled reading the coverage of *Joe Turner* and being moved by Bishop's vow to build relationships with directors of color and bring them onto LCT's stages. I asked where he was in that process now.

Bishop began his response by reminding us of his commitment to LCT3, a smaller second-stage facility that was, at that time, under construction. LCT3, he said, would focus on new plays and provide more opportunities for emerging artists. He didn't quite look at me, but he *was* looking out at 70 young directors from all over the world, when he concluded, "You know—it's quite challenging to direct on our main stages here. Especially in the Beaumont. It's a *very* difficult space."

He went on to the next question.

I remember being stunned, and then second-guessing that feeling, having trouble processing what I thought I'd heard. I turned it over in my mind. A few days later, I went backstage at the Beaumont—the larger of LCT's two main stages—to see the puppets for *War Horse* (co-directed, by the way, by Marianne Elliot, one of only three women credited with directing shows in that space in the first two decades of the 21st century). When I'd seen the show the week before, I'd been thrilled by its inventiveness, its epic scale. Now, touching the lifeless puppets hanging in the wings, I felt diffusely sad.

Ten years after Sher's *Joe Turner*, LCT has indeed diversified their larger pool of artists by regularly employing female artists and artists of color at LCT3—almost entirely on small-scale new plays focusing on the experiences of women and people of color. As far as I'm able to tell, Bishop has put a Black director—indeed, any director of color—on his main stages only three times since 2009. In the Beaumont, George C. Wolfe directed John Guare's *A Free Man of Color* in 2010, and in the smaller Newhouse, Lileana Blain-Cruz directed *Pipeline* (2017) and Saheem Ali helmed *The Rolling Stone* (2019). All three were new plays centered on the experience of African or African American characters, with predominately Black casts. This is a far cry from Bishop's claim that directors of color should have

UNSTABLE GROUND

full access to the cannon on the most prominent stages. And then, according to LCT's website, there have been no productions helmed by female directors in the "difficult" Beaumont since 2004.

⁓

I think of Alejandro sometimes. I think about how he, a fair-skinned Mexican man, was cast as Othello, without conversation or analysis—especially confounding due to the presumed whiteness of all his other castings. Was it surprising that the message he absorbed was: "you are allowed to be Black, and you are allowed to be white, but you are not allowed to be yourself"?

On twitter, I discovered the podcast "White Adjacent," created by a half Iranian, half white American guy. Every episode is an interview with a different mixed-race Iranian American. The guests describe experiences of being Americans who are not Black and are not white, who—like Alejandro and like me—may often benefit from being perceived as closer to whiteness, and also sometimes be penalized for our perceived distance from it. "We are all the same" can be especially seductive for those of us who are "white-adjacent," weaving the fantasy of inclusion while separating us from our own complex truth, our own history.

My IPP classroom at Madrona had blond Laurel and Kate, whose Spumoni sweatshirts I admired; it also had two different Asian girls named Lia whose houses I went to for sleepovers and another Asian girl named Rie who had a hyphenated last name even longer than mine. I remember a few Jewish kids, a few mixed-race kids, a girl whose family had immigrated from Ethiopia, and one African-American boy who dressed like an adult and was scrupulously academically excellent; my main memory of him is my intense feeling of competitive frustration at his perfect test scores and how he made it impossible for me to consistently be the class's top student. My parents remember the classroom as feeling "diverse"; I remember it as mostly feeling white and white-adjacent. My parents and I have the same memory of the "Regular" classrooms: that they were predominately African-American.

At the time, I had a vague conception that there was Black and there was white, so I thought of myself as white. But as I went on to middle and high school, I keenly felt the moments—increasingly frequent as I grew into less of a child, more of a young woman—where I was treated as an exotic object; it was not unusual for strangers to comment on my darker skin tone, my prominent eyebrows, my curves. In most of the schools I attended, there were two poles of popularity and coolness—a white one, to which I had torturous proximity but never belonging or acceptance, and a Black one, to which I felt I had no relationship at all. Though I felt both groups to be slightly hostile, I agonized only over the white one, circling in hopes of making some kind of contact. My *Seventeen* magazines showed thin, athletic white girls just like the ones at school, and I longed to be like them.

After 9/11, it got even harder to imagine myself as white. I was pulled out of the airport line for extra screening. Once I was standing on a corner in downtown Kansas City talking on the phone when a group of men crossed the street to walk very close to me, yelling "Go back to where you came from!"

When I lived in Manhattan, it became a running joke that I could get into any cab in the city and the cab driver would speak to me in their native language, insisting I was from wherever they were from. Pakistani, Cuban, Moroccan, Bolivian, Greek—it didn't matter. They all wanted, loudly, to claim me. I never liked this experience; I remember feeling irritated that all these strange men wanted to tell me who I was. I think now that it was also rubbing against my internal construction of whiteness—the place in me that had always felt white, perhaps because there didn't seem to be an alternative, because I felt closer to "white" than to "Black"—but also perhaps because I wanted to be good, I wanted to be right, I wanted to fit in... and that meant wanting to be white.

It wasn't a construction I had assembled, but one that had been handed down to me. This is a main tenet of the immigrant experience in this country—to align yourself with whiteness in order to be valued. The whiteness of immigrant groups has been litigated—quite literally—with sometimes devastating consequences. In 1922, after Indian nationals were deemed ineligible for US Citizenship on the basis of "racial difference" (although the court agreed that they were, technically, "Caucasian," it felt they did not fit the "common sense" definition of whiteness), some individuals were actually de-naturalized, losing land and property they had purchased. Jews were always classified as "white," but Armenians, like Indians, were more complicated—though, after a certain amount of litigation, we were eventually allowed to move from being "Asian" or "yellow" to being "free white persons."

So, Jews and Armenians reached towards whiteness and, at least legally, succeeded. And part of the compact of whiteness is defining yourself in opposition to Blackness, as not-Black. As Toni Morrison notes in her slender, stunning book on this subject, *Playing in the Dark: Whiteness and the Literary Imagination*, when America, as a young nation, sought to define itself "the process of organizing American coherence through a distancing Africanism became the operative mode of a new cultural hegemony."

To be recruited into whiteness is to agree to a non-study of self. We collude with the argument against noticing complexity, we agree to be neutral and invisible so that we may join the project of attending to the problem of the other. My grandparents understood this bargain. The Armenian rugs went to the second floor of the house; wall-to-wall carpeting was laid in the areas that would be seen by visitors, including the kitchen and bathroom. Their first daughter grew up speaking Armenian, but the youngest, my mother, never learned it. When that oldest daughter fell in love with a Cambodian man, my grandfather was so disappointed that he gathered his other two daughters to him and laid out a hierarchy of acceptable types of husband; it had American-born Apostolic Armenians at the top and Black men at the bottom.

Based on these stories, my grandparents are a confusing hybrid. They aspired to a certain kind of whiteness—they wanted to be prosperous, modern, American, accepted. They understood that to be white, they needed to hide their non-white parts—the rugs, the language—and they needed to be opposed to Blackness. But they were never interested in actually diminishing their Armenian-ness. They managed to both aspire to whiteness *and* retain their belief in Armenian superiority—a twisting balance that I wish I could talk to them about now that I understand it better than I did during their lifetimes.

⸻

Hopefully it is not too late to mention how much I loved Sher's previous LCT production, *The Light in the Piazza*—so much that I saw it twice. The luminous, timeless, "panoramic fluidity" (per *New York Magazine*'s review) of Sher's direction of Adam Guettel's beautiful musical was completely transporting. Images from the production still ring in my eyes and ears, I can feel where I was sitting in the (difficult) Beaumont as Kelli O'Hara's voice washed over me. In this production, the poetry and the shimmering beauty worked completely for me, transporting me into the Italian vacation of a Midwestern

American girl and her mom. It brought me—decidedly *not* a white, Midwestern American girl—into contact with the ways we really *are* all the same—when we are strangers far from home, curious about words in a foreign tongue, longing for connection. The production felt, to me, like it was able to universalize without obliterating.

I can still sing the songs from my fifth grade play after all these years because theater is—or can be—transporting and powerful. It can shape our images of what is, and of what is possible—for better or for worse. In the case of Sher's *Joe Turner*, for me, it was the later. The production performed an embrace of Blackness while reifying whiteness in its imagery and its point of view. The totalizing, post-racial, pro-progress narrative of the production erased the devastating sweep of American history (the experiences of Wilson's characters), the depressing reality of the American present (the deep inequities in LCT and Broadway's hiring practices), and the uncertain state of the American future (what would turn out to be our country's response to the Obama presidency).

A few weeks after my dad and I went to see *Joe Turner*, there was another piece in the *Times* about the production. It seemed that during his presidential campaign, Barack Obama had promised his wife Michelle that once it was all over he would take her to a Broadway show. Accordingly, after an intimate dinner in the Village, the First Couple attended the May 30th performance of August Wilson's masterwork, *Joe Turner's Come and Gone*, directed by Bartlett Sher. Oh, how I wish I had been in the audience that night. One woman who *was* there wrote into the Lincoln Center Theater website to say how powerful the experience was; that the play and Obama's historic presidency felt like bookends on the civil rights struggle. Another audience member wrote that she "felt the energy from the audience and the occasion meld into one," until everyone in the theater was, indeed, "shining like new money"—no gold glitter required. Although, that was there, too.

I wonder what our then-President said to his wife, flying home from their date on Air Force One—she, the descendant of slaves, and possibly also of slave owners; he, the descendant of white middle America and a Kenyan exchange student. Did he feel like a bookend? Or did he feel, like Herald Loomis, covered in the cleansing blood of the struggle, fortified with his song, balancing in that bittersweet tension between the audacious hope for a seismic shift and the tenacious knowledge of just how long the road, how great the cost?

When I returned to these essays to revise them for publication in this book, I started with this one. I was relieved to find that my analysis of Sher's glittery sheen on Wilson's ending felt as true as when I wrote it. *Joe Turner* has a happy ending; Herald Loomis is reunited with his wife and his song. In the same moment, this reunion gives him what he's been searching for and sends him running, shining with blood, away from everything he's ever known and loved, into an uncertain future. The final image is glorious, ecstatic. To throw gold glitter on something so multivalent diminishes its power—and fails to imagine what we really need, as a nation, to heal, to hope. I knew this ten years ago when I saw the production and began writing about it, and I know it now.

Then something interesting happened. I kept reading. The other essays in the book were also full of interesting, complex ideas. And inevitably, in the final paragraph of each one—sometimes in the final sentence—I tied things up neatly. A cheerfully poetic summation, a calming turn of phrase, a reassurance, a smile. I had started the book by railing against gold glitter, and had then thrown gold glitter all over it. And as we in the theater know so well, glitter sticks. You can scrub your hands, even take a shower, and you'll still find it sparkling on your pillow in the morning.

This was a distressing realization.

And then, how terrifying to *publish a book*. A book is not live theater. It lives, long past the final curtain, locking me forever into the imperfect gesture of this moment.

I am not alone, of course. It is remarkable how often a human being advocating against a thing will actually perform or encourage that very thing in the course of their advocacy. It is common to hear people with passionately held beliefs about the sacredness of life advocate for policies that would cause harm to many living beings. Public discourse about making the world safer often employs language and strategies that feel violent. And the aesthetic of a play's production can vigorously resist the ideas and values at the heart of that play.

I promise I will not do this in every essay—describe what it used to be about, and what it's about now. But it feels important in this one because of how thoroughly I undermined my own project. I set out to trouble the notion of happy endings—to interrogate them—and, in doing so, insistently replicated their most perilous potential. I found that the work I had to do in my process of revision was precisely the work I'd wished Sher had done—the work of the blues, forging the only honest kind of happy ending out of a cacophonous embrace of pain and beauty, blood and dirt and light.

It has been ten years since I sat in the audience for Sher's *Joe Turner*—ten years, enough time for a whole new installment of the Century Cycle, if only August Wilson were around to write it. I have something now that I didn't have then—a tiny bit of perspective on that feeling Bart Sher theorized we were all feeling in 2009—the sense that a seismic shift was coming.

When I first wrote the essay, I wonder if I was angry about the comparison of 1911 to 2009 because I wanted to reject it. I *knew* what was coming for Wilson's characters. I knew that the next five, fifteen, twenty five years would see The Great

Migration, yes, but also the rise of the KKK, the peak of Jim Crow, terror lynchings, Red Summer, voter disenfranchisement. To me, looking back from the future, those years looked hard. I did not, however, know what was coming for us—Americans in 2009, feeling the sense that maybe everything was changing.

I did not want to believe that the decade following 2009 would be similar to the decade following 1911. And yet.

In this sense, my rejection of the comparison was optimistic.

Sitting here in 2019, I can feel myself longing for a shimmering, poetic version of my favorite Wilson play that is also honest, that can hold all the pain of the past and all the despair of the present. I need, more than ever, to believe that a seismic shift is possible. I don't want deep naturalism. I do want the furniture to float. Can I have the floating furniture without the gold glitter? Is there a version that embraces the luminosity *and* the grit?

Part of the story of my childhood is an intimate experience of segregation resulting from a program of voluntary busing intended to make the system more equal and yet failing spectacularly. The racialized juxtaposition of "IPP" and "Regular," side by side without comment or explanation, was a performance of the violence of systems—the results of institutional racism, redlining, income disparity—so legible that it was clear even to ten year old eyes.

I am grateful for having been part of this failed experiment. I could easily have spent my childhood, and longer, shielded from these truths.

The truth inside our school was that we were separate and unequal. Another part of the truth was that I loved being a student there. I loved playing tether ball at recess, I loved the annual read-a-thon, I loved Ms. Hawkins and, especially, Ms. Tegenfeldt, who had our class over to her house for a sleepover at the end of the year. I guess teachers probably aren't allowed to do that anymore. In Ms. Tegenfeldt's class, I wrote a story called "Minnesota, Here We Come!" about a multi-generational Armenian family traveling from Mexico to Minnesota in a covered wagon. This awkward, earnest attempt to fit what I understood of my family's story into the version of American history I was learning in school reads as a bizarre Laura Ingalls Wilder fan fiction mashup with Armenian names and a very shaky understanding of North American geography. But it's also the last time in all my years of schooling that I remember writing anything related to my personal history. It would be years before I was able to peel back the chorus of "we are all the same" enough to try and find my own song.

Madrona tried to remedy the fissure of segregation in its student body by hiring artists to make a play with us; the result for me was to come into more conscious contact with the fissure. The play provided no remedy—but without the experience of performing the division, I don't know if, all these years later,

I would remember as clearly what it felt like. "We are all the same" was an unhelpful ending—it shunted me back into the system with no tools to critique it—but the play was effective to the extent that it seared in my memory an image of the rupture it aimed to erase.

I still remember the feeling of standing on stage during the climactic "San Andreas fault" sequence—I was all the way stage left, near the heavy velvet curtains, in the middle of a sea of ten-year-old bodies, divided into two groups, facing off. We yelled across the divide, "Why won't you listen me?," building in volume as we'd rehearsed, and then, on a cue from the piano, we screamed in unison, "Earthquake!" We convulsed our small bodies, limbs flailing, voices vibrating, before falling one by one to the ground. I remember lying there in the silence, my heart beating hard against the wooden floor of the cafeteria-auditorium stage, feeling a sea of other bodies around me, all felled by the same force. There would be no seismic change in daily life at Madrona—but somewhere in me, the plates shifted.

Take It From The Breakdown

Since I was a small child, spaces where audiences could gather—from my living room to the elementary school cafeteria to the college black box—have always called to me. "Make something for people here!" they seem to whisper. I've never once wanted to make movies or television. I am hopelessly addicted to the live.

It's been strange and different, making this book, this thing that lives quietly on a page, where I can't see my audience. I keep trying to figure out my relationship to you. Where are you sitting?

There have been a few times in my career when I've directed a "fourth wall play"—the kind of play that behaves as if there is an imaginary additional wall of the room between the players and us, the audience. But most plays I love exist in the epic theatrical world where our live presence is needed for the play to happen. Characters speak or sing directly to us, they make confessions and ask questions. There is a complicity between performer and audience that is necessary for the work to proceed. In traditional epic theater (Shakespeare, Brecht, the Greeks), spectators are often assumed to be impartial observers—present, but outside the world of the play. When Isabella asks, "To whom should I complain?" she may be asking for our empathy, but not our assistance. But some plays put everyone in the same room. These plays may "cast" the audience (as asylum inmates in *Marat/Sade*) or may address us as ourselves, that is, as an audience watching a play (*What the Constitution Means to Me*). My favorite in this genre is *Hedwig and The Angry Inch*, the iconic glam-punk musical with music and lyrics by Stephen Trask and a book by John Cameron Mitchell, which casts us as the audience of a rock show.

Hedwig tells the story of a boy named Hansel who, desperate to escape Communist East Berlin, has a sex change operation in order to marry an American GI. The operation is botched, and Hansel—now Hedwig—is left with "an angry inch" of flesh between her legs. Hedwig does make it to the US and, after her marriage dissolves, she falls hard for an American teenager, Tommy. When he betrays her, stealing the songs they wrote together, Hedwig pours her grief and rage into her music, playing gigs at low-rent venues near the large arenas where Tommy, now a star, is performing. Every so often she opens the back door of the venue to let Tommy's bright lights and stadium-sized cheers spill in.

Her band, The Angry Inch, includes her new husband, Yitzhak, who sings backup and silently shoulders the abuse Hedwig heaps on him. It seems to be just another rock show, until things start to unravel, and we begin to realize that this night may be different from all other nights.

The show follows a dramaturgical arc that I've come to think of as "Hedwig Structure." In Hedwig Structure, the conceit is that there is a live performance that we, the audience, have come to see. The performance begins according to plan—but at some point, things begin to go wrong. There are surprises, unexpected events that the performer(s) must respond to. At first it seems possible to get back on track, but as things go further off the rails, the performers falter, and ultimately are forced to abandon their rehearsed set-list to discover something new right there in front of us, in collaboration with us.

When the show works well—as it did on a balmy August night in 1998 when I sat spellbound in the Jane Street Theatre, watching John Cameron Mitchell in the title role during *Hedwig*'s initial off-Broadway run—the whole room arrives together at the recognition that Hedwig is at once freak and rock star, corrupt and innocent, broken and whole, she and he. At the end of the show, Hedwig and the band sing ecstatically "Lift up your hands!," and that night all of us in the audience did lift up our hands, celebrating Hedwig, celebrating us all.

When I got the chance to direct *Hedwig*, I was thrilled—a punk rock musical love story! I rarely get to work on something that offers so much unbridled joy. The production, in a tiny black box at the (now dearly departed) Perishable Theatre, was so successful that we were offered the chance to re-mount it the following year with Trinity Repertory Company, in a cavernous former bank just down Empire Street in downtown Providence, RI.

It was in rehearsing the re-mount that I started to find myself drawn not only to the joy in *Hedwig*, but also to the terror. Yes, I'd always known that Hedwig was German. I'd caught the glib little jokes about ovens. I saw the metaphorical significance of the cat-and-mouse game our heroine plays throughout the show with Yitzhak, a Croatian Jew. I knew all of this, but genocide had seemed to me the dark backstory, mere set-up for the punk rock romance to come. As I got closer, I saw that it was less the backstory than the engine—the terror behind the power, the oppression behind the freedom, the losses behind the choices—fueling both the music and the narrative.

⌒

I don't know much about how or why my grandparents and great-grandparents came to this country. I only know that they came—from Turkey, from Austria, Romania, Ukraine—and that they came in time. On the Armenian side, just before the massacres during World War I at the hands of the Turks; on the Jewish side, decades before World War II. No one in my family ever told me a personal story of the forced marches or the concentration camps. And I never asked what it was like to watch, from the Eastern coast of the United States of America, newscasts announcing the obliteration of the people and places they'd left behind. And yet, it seems to me that the stories they did tell were steeped in the dust and ashes of these defining events. My cultural history is, at least in part (a part that sometimes stands in for the whole), a story of astronomical loss. I remember the books I read as a child—*Number the Stars, The Road From Home*. If I read non-genocide-themed stories about what it meant to be Jewish or Armenian, I don't remember them. Eventually, I learned to dread these books (and movies and plays). Far from offering catharsis or healing, they barely even registered as history—they felt more like, as Delaware First Nations playwright Daniel David Moses put it, "dancing around a wound."

Where is this wound in my body? How are these dual histories of genocide contained in me? In the veins of this very first-world, upper-middle-class American anatomy, buried like an underground river, runs the memory of trauma from another time, another place. I can feel it, but not see it—a rushing pressure that I know is there, fueling the system from deep underground. What is in that river? The unconfessed nightmares of my great-grandparents, the imagined screams of families just like mine? One and a half million Armenians during and after World War I. Six million Jews during World War II. Is that all in me? I don't know if my great-grandparents, my grandparents, my parents, ever grieved these losses. I know that this is my own dark backstory—and sometimes I wonder if, like the terror in *Hedwig*, it is also the engine fueling my narrative.

John Cameron Mitchell has called *Hedwig* "a play about division and duality." He was inspired by a story in Plato's *Symposium* that describes an ancient bisection dealt to humans by the Gods as punishment for defiance, tearing each of us in two, and leaving us in a lifelong search for our other half. From the opening number, the rousing "Tear Me Down," where Hedwig literally dresses as the Berlin wall—"standing before you in the divide between East and West, Slavery and Freedom, Man and Woman"—the show repeatedly introduces elements of trauma and division. Germany, perpetrator of the greatest global trauma of the twentieth century, is punished, in ancient fashion, by being split in two. To escape the divided city of Berlin at the center of the divided country of Germany, Hedwig accepts both a surgical division (of her genitals) and an alteration of her gender identity. "To be free," her mother tells her, "one must give up a little part of oneself."

In the swift and singable middle section of the show—"Angry Inch," "Wig in a Box," "Wicked Little Town"—Hedwig has her botched operation, makes it to America, is abandoned by her husband Luther, falls for Tommy, transforms him from a pimply teenager to a confident musician, and then is abandoned by him, too. A heartbroken Hedwig subsequently re-enacts her own double-edged escape/division by offering to marry the drag queen Yitzhak and bring him to America, "on the condition that a wig never touch [his] head again." Throughout the show, Yitzhak looks longingly at Hedwig's costumes and wigs, even going so far as to try one on when he thinks she isn't looking, for which Hedwig publicly shames him. As an irate Hedwig slips into recollections of her ill-fated love affair with Tommy, she yells at her band to improvise. Clearly, Tommy was *not* on the set-list. But it's a part of her story that, tonight, she feels compelled to tell.

I can't say this about any other show I've directed, but I would have watched every single performance of *Hedwig*. There are so few perfect human-made things in the world, but, along with peanut M&Ms and salt and vinegar Kettle Chips, I would count the final three songs of *Hedwig and The Angry Inch*. As things begin to go off the rails, Hedwig tries to take refuge in Yitzhak, the husband she has spent the entire show demeaning and insulting. Yitzhak rejects her. As they segue into "Hedwig's Lament/ Exquisite Corpse," Hedwig breaks down, ripping off her glam-rock drag, including her huge trademark wig, as well as the shorter shag wig she wears beneath it. She smashes the tomatoes she's used to stuff her bra and collapses to the ground, a seedy, pulpy, ragged, bare-headed mess. We hear Tommy's voice from next door, distant and echoing, and then suddenly closer; stadium-sized cheers wash over us, and the two spaces seem, through the magic of theater, to become one. We, the audience, are in both the tiny dive bar with Hedwig and the huge arena with Tommy—and, as the actor playing Hedwig picks himself up from the floor, we understand that it is now the body of Tommy. There is a silver cross shining on his forehead and a boyish confidence in the set of his shoulders; he steps to the microphone to the roar of the crowd and the opening piano notes of the "Wicked Little Town" reprise. Tommy, through Hedwig's body, asks Hedwig's forgiveness. As she sang to him so long ago, he now sings back to her, "When you've got no other choice, you know you can follow my voice." Tommy smiles gently and turns away. The crowd swells and then fades. The actor turns back to the mic, Hedwig once again. We too are dropped back into the room and into our own bodies. Hedwig, broken, whole, picks up her wig, offers it to Yitzhak. Freedom. She sings the soaring anthem "Midnight Radio," and we lift up our hands.

Many fans now know *Hedwig* not from seeing it onstage but through the 2001 film, in which Mitchell reprises his role as Hedwig while another actor plays Tommy Gnosis. And though Michael Pitt's Tommy is the pitch-perfect embodiment of emo teen heartthrob, the literalization of the two characters in two different bodies makes the ecstatic union of the live event impossible. In a live audience, we participate in the rupture of the form that occurs when the narrative goes off the rails; like Hedwig, we both break and are broken, and then we come back together, changed.

The sequence of the final three songs, like all of the most frustrating and rewarding feats of live theater, requires intimate collaboration—in this case, between lighting, sound and costume design, live musicians, props, make-up, wigs, and stage management. I remember the detailed negotiations to determine the level of ripeness for a tomato that is conducive to both safe bra-stuffing while performing a rock show, and to effective smashing and smearing at the end of it. Likewise, there were experiments with silver makeup to figure out what would work best for the actor to locate and apply quickly while crouched on the ground in the dark. The sequence from "Exquisite Corpse" to Tommy's "Wicked Little Town" had to be teched and re-teched so often that every time we started again the actor playing Hedwig took to asking, "So—take it from the breakdown?"

Attending to the technical minutiae removed none of the magic for me. In fact—and this is not always, or even usually, the case—even dismantled, even in pieces that didn't fully function, the sequence destroyed me every time. Each time I felt the agony of division, the longing for reunion, the painful recognition that we are separated only from ourselves, that the lover we long for can only be located by embracing the terrifying truths within. Tommy, who has stolen Hedwig's song, returns it to her as a transformative apology. Hedwig, who has used Yitzhak's trauma and his devotion as an analgesic for her own injury, offers her husband the chance to be both free *and* whole—something that she herself was never given. This moment is so charged because Yitzhak's freedom has been placed in relationship to a series of personal and historical narratives of violence and trauma. In the diaspora of trauma, the victim and the perpetrator are those slashed-apart halves of one soul, rolling along, smashing into each other in an attempt to reunite. When Hedwig hands her wig to Yitzhak, she is doing her best to break the cycle. She defies the myth of division—"to be free, one must give up a little part of oneself"—and ushers in a new era of possibility.

It can't be a coincidence that my second-favorite use of Hedwig Structure is in Lisa Kron's beautiful and devastating *2.5 Minute Ride,* which casts the audience as viewers of an imaginary slide show documenting a trip she took with her ailing father to Auschwitz, where his parents died. I've never worked on a full production of *2.5 Minute Ride,* but I did direct it in a staged reading for Yom Hashoah, Holocaust Remembrance Day, several years ago. The role of "Lisa"—avatar of the playwright, and the only role in this one-actor play—was played by a brilliant, hilarious actress named Veronika. Veronika is German—not a German Jew, but the daughter of tall, blond German immigrants who lived through the events of WW II in their homeland before coming to the US as young adults. We had discussed the complex identity intersections in advance, but I was unprepared for the surge of sudden, strong feelings that arrived on the afternoon of our rehearsal. Waves of rage and grief coursed through me. As I gave direction, shaping the performance that an auditorium full of Jewish people would come to see that evening as an act of remembrance and to honor those lost, I felt simultaneously deeply conflicted and deeply moved at the standing-in of Veronika's body for Lisa's.

During the talkback after the performance, Veronika and I sat side by side and talked about our personal stories. For the first time, I spoke publicly about wanting to find my way to stories that would reckon with the ancestral trauma on both sides of my heritage. I was washed with a clarity I'd never felt before: I can tell these stories and survive. I *must* tell these stories and survive.

Was it the body of a German woman that gifted me this freedom? What I mean is, was this gift of freedom made possible by the embodiment of the Jewish experience by a tall, blond German woman?

I wonder how this moment has stuck with Veronika. I emailed her to see if we could talk about it, but she was in the middle of rehearsing a demanding show and living in a new city and caring for her young daughter. She suggested we check in again after her show closed. But then the show opened and closed and I didn't reach back out.

I'm not sure why.

I'm also not entirely sure I can finish this essay without talking to her.

What did I say? "The lover we long for can only be located by embracing the terrifying truths within"? Is that really what I mean?

Why is it that Hedwig Structure works so well for telling the story of trauma in general, and genocide in particular?

In *2.5 Minute Ride,* Lisa's father is deeply in touch with how thin the line is between Germans who committed atrocities during WWII and those who lost their lives to those atrocities. "If it weren't for the good fortune of being born a Jew, I might have become a Nazi," he says. He tells the story of interrogating a Gestapo agent during his service in WWII, "I looked across my desk at this man and knew he could have been me… I knew how very much alike we were and that he, in a very real sense, was my brother."

How well does anyone who sees *Hedwig* remember the moment before Hansel becomes Hedwig? Have you seen it? Do you remember? Young Hansel is offered a package of gummy bears by his fawning would-be lover, Luther Robinson. Hansel looks at the gummies and sees in them a vision: "Panting faces of every imaginable color, creed, and non-Aryan origin, fogging up the bag like the windows of a Polish bathhouse. It's only a shower. Absolute power!" He drops the candy and flees. The next day, he returns, accepting the pile of candy and the role of Luther's lover, along with his own power, his own sexuality, his own capacity for violence. After telling this story Hedwig strikes a triumphant pose to the first few bars of "Deutschland Uber Alles"—a portion of the song closely identified with the Nazi regime—and sets the events of the play in motion.

We *know* what's at risk. We know what our capacities are. History tells us. The blood in our veins tells us. We know what dark terror runs through our underground rivers. But if, like Hansel, the only way to grasp our own freedom is to embrace the dark power inside… wouldn't we do it?

I think -

I think we would -

I think I would.

I know I would.

I pray with every Jewish-Christian-non-denominational fiber of my being that I never end up on that side of the wall, in a place hard enough that I have to discover what I could become. I know what I am capable of because I know what we are all capable of. Everything—the worst—beyond the worst—the most unimaginable—*that is inside me.*

Every year on April 24, the anniversary of the beginning of the Armenian genocide, and on Yom Hashoah (which, depending on the Hebrew calendar, often falls in that same week in April), people, including me, post versions of a quote inspired by Greek poet Dinos Christianopoulos, "They tried to bury us. They didn't know we were seeds."

This is the survivor mythology: existence is resistance; survival is triumph. And still we rise!

It is beautiful, and it is true. It is also totalizing. It recommits us to the binary—victim/perpetrator, innocent/guilty—instead of allowing for the fact that survival is not just heroic, but also messy. And that sometimes the messiness of survival can generate in us the capacity to perpetrate, to reenact our own trauma and even revisit it on others. Without seeing this terrifying

THERE MUST BE HAPPY ENDINGS

truth, can we ever really see ourselves?

The gift of *Hedwig* is that the power of our live witnessing knocks the binary narrative off the rails. In the wreckage of the crash, a space opens for the necessary acknowledgement of harm. Once Tommy acknowledges what he has done to Hedwig, Hedwig can surrender her identification with the role of victim and acknowledge the ways she has acted as a perpetrator. Only then can she begin to remedy the harm she's caused to Yitzhak. Because Hedwig and Tommy are played by the same actor onstage, we are able to see how one body contains many experiences and possibilities and how any one of us can choose to break the cycle—all it takes is a willingness to hear the song of an exiled part of ourselves.

Even I wouldn't argue that a play is a political remedy. In the realm of material reality, we do, in fact, need acknowledgement from the perpetrator. Denial of harm is an extremely effective method for continuance of harm. I can feel this starkly in the two halves of my personal history. The Armenian half has the continuing trauma of an ongoing international debate about the nature of the harm, including sustained and vigorous denial by the perpetrator. The Jewish half has the benefit of a powerful and continuing international recognition of harm, including sustained efforts by the perpetrator to offer reparations for that harm.

But too often political remedy—acknowledgment, reparations,

regime change—is unavailable. And I do think live performance has the capacity to do something nothing else can do. In the intimacy of creative, collaborative risk-taking, in the vulnerability of the breakdown, in going off the rails together, there can be a real healing in a manufactured experience.

I think that's true.

And it also feels incomplete.

In a 1999 *New York Times* interview, John Cameron Mitchell said that he wanted Hedwig to be post-sexuality and post-drag, "more about gender and love generally." Ever since the Obama-era rhetoric extolling a "post-racial" America, I have an allergic reaction to the prefix. But revisiting it in the context of Mitchell's words, I can see that the "after" of "post" could indicate not that we are finished with something, but that it is no longer uncontested. Once set in motion—colonialism, war, racial categorization— we are forever changed, we are rocked by these forces, they shape our forward motion. A post-sexuality, post-drag narrative allows that we have been irrevocably shaped by a binary view of sexuality and gender and asks what new identities might be forged in its wake.

I wonder, then, if *Hedwig* might also desire to be post-genocide and post-trauma, more about violence and power and grief generally, about what is possible and maybe impossible after we survive or perpetrate an atrocity—reparation, forgiveness, release.

Another prefix comes to mind, especially after the 2014 Broadway revival of the show, when Hedwig was heralded by many as "a trans icon." In a split, binary world, the only option is to be either a man or a woman. "Trans," as a preposition, means across, through, over, beyond. A binary view of trans identity allows for a transition from male to female—a journey from one side to the other. But *Hedwig* reaches for a place on the other side of the binary—outside or beyond this conception of gender and selfhood, integrated, whole.

So, then, trans-genocidal: to go to the other side of trauma—or beyond. To escape the binary—genocide or no genocide—victim or perpetrator—and transition into the painful truth of everyday erasure and re-birth: the countless attempts of the culture to stamp us out, the countless ways we collude with this erasure and visit it on others, and also the insistent impulses of resistance and subversion and survival.

Hedwig gives us a kind of radical trans-belonging across borders and binaries, a punk-rock alchemy so incendiary that it burns away even the need for sameness and difference. In that crucible, it is our live witnessing that turns the event from disaster to opportunity. Our participation transforms it from flameout to rebirth. By going with the performers as they abandon the set-list and careen into unknown territory, we rehearse the courage needed to encounter the unexpected, the dangerously complex. We are reminded that it is possible to fall apart and then get back up again with capacities we never had before. We travel beyond an imagined unity, beyond completion, into the chaotic multiplicity of true togetherness.

And then we leave the theater separately. We leave with whatever dark backstory we came in with. None of it is dissolved or resolved. We come together, and then we leave alone.

I so badly want to give you that feeling, here.

I'm worried it's not possible, though, without being live in a room together.

This essay was so hard to write. I stopped in the middle, which I didn't know was the middle. I thought maybe it was the end. Even so, I didn't think I could finish. I lit candles and blew them out. I drove around in the rain. I sat in the car crying, unable to find the energy to climb the stairs and put the key in the lock and stare at the screen and try again.

The distance between us is painful—I can feel it, the torn-apart place—and it takes work for me to reconcile it, to hold us here in the tension: in one hand, the reality of our separateness, in the other, the reality of our interconnection.

It is both terror and revelation. We are separate. We are inseparable. We will damage each other. We will damage ourselves. At any moment—at every moment—it is in our power to reunite.

I careened off the rails in my writing, but only because I wanted to find you so badly, because I believe in what is possible between us. I believe that the kind of intimacy I long for with you only becomes possible through shared risk, a collision with something real and really, truly, actually difficult. The punk-rock hope for a broken-but-joined knowing. The glitter and light, the sweet throb of the bass in the floor, the pulsing joy of lifting up our hands, together.

Wolf at the Door

For years the word *wolf* couldn't be spoken aloud in our household. It had to be spelled, even by me, when confessing my nightly terrors to my parents: "I'm scared of the W-O-L-F."

At the time I was devoted to my orange and brown plastic Fisher Price record player, and was particularly fond of playing records that came with follow-along picture books: "When it's time to turn the page, you will hear the sound of the chime, like this—" *ding*! I experienced most of the Disney pantheon this way before I ever saw the movies.

There was one record that I loved to hate and played over and over: a Sterling Holloway-narrated recording of Prokofiev's *Peter and The Wolf.* The three slow, menacing French horns that signaled the Wolf's approach made my pulse quicken and my limbs constrict. I could feel the threat of what might be out there, in that darkening place where the meadow meets the forest—the threat Peter's grandfather warns him of, a warning he does not heed.

As an adult, re-visiting the recording—which someone has helpfully uploaded to YouTube—I was surprised to find that the story ends with a triumphant Peter capturing the Wolf, assisted by his other animal friends, and then carting him off to the zoo. Peter marches proudly, now less of a boy and more of a man. The happy ending apparently made little impression on me. The part I remember vividly is pre-capture, when the Wolf chases and catches the Duck—a cluster of worried oboes—devouring her in one gulp. (Side note: I loved to feed the mallards at Greenlake, a park close to our home in Seattle, and my first word was "duck"—so the tragic fate of Peter's Duck may have hit particularly close to home.) The score ends with a faint reprise of the Duck's oboe theme, which is overtaken by Peter's music as the victory parade marches on. Prokofiev's original narration concludes, "And perhaps, if you listen very carefully, you will hear the Duck quacking inside the Wolf, because the Wolf, in his hurry, had swallowed her alive." The End!

In the record I had, though, which was produced by Disney, the final piece of narration has been changed to interpret the oboe reprise not as the Duck calling from inside the Wolf, but as the Bird's sad memory of his lost playmate. Then, suddenly, the Duck re-appears! And the Bird, overcome, rejoices: "Oh, you're not dead! You hid in the hollow tree! … Now Peter can go hunting whenever he likes, and we'll all live happily forever and ever after." The End!

I don't remember why I was fascinated by this record, why I listened to it over and over. Was I testing myself, checking to see if I'd still be scared of the Wolf? (I always was.) Was I testing the story, to make sure that the Wolf always got captured in the end? (It always did.) Did I *like* the record? Or did I hate it? Was the experience of listening wholly disturbing, or was there something pleasurable about the terror I knew I would find there? Did my fascination have to do with the unsettled darkness of the music lurking just beneath the Disney-ified narration?

At some point between ages four and nine, I transferred my fixation from the Fisher Price record player to a handheld tape deck of indeterminate brand, and from Disney Read-Along Records to musical theater cast albums. The first soundtracks I played were from the movie versions of Rogers and Hammerstein classics: *South Pacific*, *The King and I*, and, especially, Julie Andrews in *The Sound of Music*. I used to rewind and replay the fifth track, "I Have Confidence," singing along, sometimes swinging my arms and running and spinning exuberantly the way Maria does in the film. In seventh grade, our music teacher, Mr. Ito, was ambitious or foolish enough to stage *West Side Story* with the Washington Middle School orchestra playing the full score. He double-cast all the main roles, so I was one of two Anitas, and that was good enough for me. My Maria was Santana Vallejos, and we spent hours together, listening to the music and talking about it. Santana had long, beautiful hair and slender arms. I remember the feeling of holding her hand during the curtain call—her palm so soft, her hold on me so firm.

By the time I was 15, I had a boom box with a CD player. Also at 15, I fell in love for the first time—although I didn't call it that, then. Liza had hazel eyes and floppy hair; she drove an Acura Integra and was a year ahead of me in school. She wanted to be a famous actress and had a particular fondness for the musical *Annie*. Or maybe it wasn't a fondness, exactly. Liza would ash her Marlboro lights into an empty Diet Pepsi can, and say, throatily, "What ever happened to Andrea McArdle?" This was pre-Google, and, as far as we knew, the little girl who had been such a huge sensation when she starred in *Annie* on Broadway was now lost to the fickle sands of pop-culture time.

In any good musical, says Stephen Schwartz (who knows from good musicals, being the author of many, including *Godspell* and *Wicked*), the main character sings an "I want" or "I wish" song in the first fifteen minutes. This song itself usually doesn't drive the action of the plot forward, but rather pauses the action to set up the desire of the leading character—which will then drive the action forward. Sometimes it's the hope for a better life ("Our Prayer" from *The Color Purple*, "Wouldn't It Be Loverly" from *My Fair Lady*) or an existential longing to fulfill a purpose ("Much More" from *The Fantasticks*, "Corner of the Sky" from Schwartz's *Pippin*). Often it's a desire to get out, to be somewhere else, exemplified by the plucky Disney heroines of my generation; I still know all the words to "Belle," "Part of Your World," and "Just Around the Riverbend"—the "I wish" songs from *Beauty and The Beast*, *The Little Mermaid*, and *Pocahontas*, respectively. Occasionally it is the literal desire for romantic love, as in "Goodnight My Someone" from *The Music Man* or the original Disney version of the genre, Snow White's

"I'm Wishing," warbled into, yes, a *wishing* well. The best "I wish" songs, the ones we are likely to leave the theater singing, or choose for karaoke night, are those that have big, ambitious longings. See: the iconic "My Shot" from *Hamilton*, in which our titular hero and his new friends, and, by proxy, the entire nation, sing about the drive to rise up, rise up, in revolution.

Desire is the force that sets things in motion; without it, nothing would ever happen. The performance artist Deb Margolin has said that desire is "our dramaturgical force." And the poet and critic Susan Stewart, in her book *On Longing*, sees all narrative as "a structure of desire." Wanting something is the first step to getting something, thus the enduring truth of musical theater dramaturgy: the more clearly we understand what the protagonist wants at the beginning, the more ardently we can root for them to get it in the end.

Stephen Sondheim, master of the meta-musical, made cheeky reference to this convention of musical theater structure in his fairy-tale mash-up *Into the Woods*, which begins with multiple characters, including Cinderella and Jack (of Beanstalk fame), singing the lyric "I wish!" repeatedly. By the end of the first act, everyone's wish is granted in familiar happily-ever-after fashion. Hooray! But then, the second act begins with an "I wish!" reprise. Predictably, the characters have all discovered some new yearning. At the show's conclusion, after the battered and bruised characters have learned their lesson about desire ("Careful the wish you make... wishes come true—not free"), in the micro-instant of space between the satisfying resolution of the big finale and the beginning of the applause, Cinderella steps forward with one last plaintive, "I wish…!" Curtain.

Into the Woods demonstrates how, in a fairy tale, "I wish" tees up the narrative for an utterly-fulfilled "happily ever after," in defiance of the reality that wishing is not something we ever stop doing—not at the beginning, the middle, or the end. The continued existence of desire—which keeps us moving forward, living—also makes a fairy-tale happy ending impossible. Desire enables narrative. Narrative requires an ending. A happy ending requires the fulfillment of desire, which is really the elimination of desire.

When "I wish" is located in its traditional position—the first or second or third song in the show—it is a safe and orderly desire, desire pointing us towards "happily ever after." Second act wishes, though, are more dangerous. They pose a threat to a happy ending. Like the Duck still trying to sing her song inside the belly of the Wolf, they remind us that desire does not die easily and happy endings are provisional at best.

Theater has a reputation for being a sanctuary for the outsider, a place where anyone who feels a little different can find community, purpose, and joy. Musical theater as a refuge and a passion for gay men in particular is not only a favorite pop-culture stereotype but also the subject of much socio-historical analysis and theorizing—on the attractions of the flamboyance and style of the musical stage, on identification with the outsize persona of the diva, on the opportunity to over-perform (and hence transgress) gendered stereotypes. This all makes good sense, but it doesn't help me understand what *I* felt, spinning around my room pretending to be Julie Andrews, or sitting in the passenger seat of Liza's Acura with my sunglasses on and the stereo cranked up. It was not the thrill of the fabulous that drew me. Rather, I think, the kind of desire found on the musical stage and in those soundtracks—huge, consuming, so powerful it must be sung—matched the size of the desire that I felt inside but feared I might never be able to express.

A friend of mine, an extraordinary singer and actress who recently came out as queer in her 40's, tells the story of the first time she encountered musical theater as a little girl growing up in the Midwest—a magical outdoor summer theater production of *Annie.* She was riveted by the scale of what she saw—a glimpse of a world where adults could be passionate, bold, ridiculous. She vowed at that moment that she would pursue musical theater so that she, too, could live in that place, where desire that was otherwise out of bounds—too large, too loud, too dangerous—was given voice, where big feelings were celebrated instead of repressed.

For those of us who feel we have to move through our lives hiding what we want, rather than risk rejection, expulsion, or even death, desire becomes an epic secret. Forced into hiding, it grows to a massive scale. A good musical allows us—all of us—to step into an imaginary world where desire can be sung out loud in a full-throated, totally embodied way; it's a safe place to live for a few hours and feel what it would be like to sing about big feelings before having to step back into lives where we must shrink and limit ourselves. Returning to listen and re-listen to a musical, then, is the opposite of re-listening to *Peter and The Wolf*—revisiting safety rather than revisiting terror.

Stacy Wolf has written beautifully about the "problem" of being a musical theater fan as well as a woman, a lesbian, and a feminist. In her books *A Problem Like Maria* and *Changed for Good*, Wolf provides feminist and queer readings of characters and relationships in musical theater ("the challenge is to identify how lesbians appear where none officially exist"!), offering that the form, from its earliest incarnations, has always contained strong homo-social and homo-erotic feelings and relationships, available to those who wish to see and feel them. She writes of the tension of taking refuge and finding joy in a form that promotes conservative values (hetero-normativity, traditional views of femininity and women's work) but also allows for empowering representations of female characters and (covert) queerness.

In *The Musical As Drama*, Scott McMillin offers that it is not only the queerness of the relationships, but "the double-coding and the subversion and the repetition" at the heart of the musical theater form that draws queer people to it. In contrast to the accepted theory, which holds the unique feature of American musical theater, starting with *Oklahoma!*, to be the integration of the songs with the book, McMillin writes that musical theater structure holds true to the disjunctive and irreverent forms of popular entertainment from which it arose. Musicals toggle between "progressive time" (the forward-moving plot points of the book) and "repetitive time" (the lyrical and musical structures of song and, sometimes, dance). What we enjoy in a musical is not the smoothness of unity, but "the crackle of difference," as the show moves between being organized by narrative (the book) and by repetition (the musical numbers). The songs, designed for pleasure, are indeed pleasurable—but also, somehow, unsettling, because they stand apart, even from the book, in which they are supposedly integrated. They point to something else, something under the surface. Then they take that under-the-surface thing and sing and dance about it, with a pleasurable yet disturbing intensity.

What is the under-the-surface thing? Does it matter? Just the suggestion of something hidden is enough to awaken in the listener a sense that the secrets onstage might be the same as the one she harbors in her own heart. When I read Stacy Wolf's analysis of Maria in *The Sound of Music* as a character who is initially coded as queer (short hair! living in a community of women! cavorting around the countryside wearing clothes made out of curtains! turning children into radical little Bohemians who sing and dance instead of sitting quietly!) and who, over the course of the show, is successfully "rehabilitated" into heterosexuality, a light went on. *Ah!* I thought. *This feels... relevant to me.*

I don't know where my queerness lived in me in the W-O-L-F days, or where exactly it was when I moved on to playing *The Sound of Music* soundtrack on repeat on my cassette player, but I know it was there. It was there when I held Santana's slender hand at the curtain call for *West Side Story;* it was certainly there when Liza and I sat in her parked car wondering about Andrea McArdle. But just like the queerness in those musicals, my queerness was coded—best friends, actresses, intimacy, art. I hid it—even, for a time, from myself.

During my college years, though, the familiar coding slowly began to fall away—for Broadway and for me. Musicals with explicitly queer content meant that it wasn't always necessary to read between the lines. *Falsettos* was on Broadway and so was a scantily-clothed Alan Cumming in the dark Donmar Warehouse revival of *Cabaret.* As a college student, I would take the bus into the city to see shows. Once I graduated, I moved there and lived in a tiny walkup in the Meatpacking district—back when they still packed meat there and I had to be careful not to splash my ankles with blood when I rode my bike over the cobblestones on my way to work. In those years, there were three shows in particular that triangulated into a mini-bucket-list of my own desire, three shows that I instantly loved and longed to direct: *Rent, Spring Awakening,* and *Hedwig and The Angry Inch.*

Sometime in the late 90's, a college friend gave me a cassette tape copy of her cast recording of *Rent* and I listened to it for the first time at the gym; I remember sitting there on the stationary bike sobbing. It wasn't just that the almost-adult me strongly related to the inevitable tension between following your dreams and paying your rent. The sparse, driving "One Song Glory" was an "I Wish" song for my generation. The song comes about fifteen minutes into the show (classic "I wish" placement) as the filmmaker Mark leaves his friend Roger in their apartment on Christmas Eve, narrating: "Close on Roger. His girlfriend April left a note saying 'we've got AIDS' before slitting her wrists in the bathroom." Roger, alone with his guitar, sings about his longing to write one great song before he dies. The driving guitar and raw vocals captured the burning intensity of both my bright anticipation—"find glory / in a song that rings true"—and the dark urgency I felt, not to wait too long to begin my life—"one song/ to redeem this empty life." The sense of impending doom and the need to create, twinned and inseparable. I knew, of course, that *Rent*'s writer and composer, Jonathan Larson, had died suddenly from an undiagnosed heart defect following the final dress rehearsal at New York Theatre Workshop. At least he'd seen it once, I thought.

In my final year of college, I ventured downtown to the Jane Street Theatre to see John Cameron Mitchell's off-Broadway musical *Hedwig and The Angry Inch*. In it, the title character tells her life story, beginning when she was Hansel—a young East German lad who is seduced by an American GI. In order to marry the soldier and start a new life in America, Hansel must become a woman—but after the sex change operation is botched, Hansel, now Hedwig, ends up alone in a trailer park in middle-America, with "an angry inch" between her legs. As Hedwig searches to discover who she is, she meets and falls for American teenager Tommy Gnosis. Hedwig's "I wish" song, "Origin of Love," describes a long-ago bedtime story, derived from a passage in Plato's *Symposium*, in which an angry god splits humans in two and leaves them always searching for their other half. Tommy, she implies, is her other half, once violently wrenched away from her, with whom reunion is inevitable—although, perhaps, equally violent.

Hedwig's story emerges in pieces as she performs her cabaret act at a dive bar with her band, The Angry Inch. Her narrative is driven—and sometimes derailed—by both her memories of desire and the desperation that overtakes her in the present moment as she shouts out the back door to Tommy, who is performing his own show at a nearby arena. But over the course of the performance, the scale of the desire subtly slides outward. We become aware not only of Hedwig's longing for Tommy to hear her, but also of her desire to really listen to the world around her and be listened to in return—not a desire for Tommy to complete her, but a recognition that her whole, damaged self fits perfectly into the universe, at this moment, completing it. As Hedwig starts to release herself to everything around her, she is finally naked before us, able to be who she/he really is, for her/him-self.

A matching his-and-hers pair of "I wish" songs kicks off *Spring*

Awakening, the rock musical set in 19ᵗʰ- century Germany and based on the play of the same name by Frank Wedekind, with a spare, darkly clever book by Steven Sater, and lush, emotional score by Duncan Sheik. "Mama Who Bore Me" begins the show with our heroine Wendla and a chorus of teenage girls lamenting their mothers' collective failure to educate them on what really matters; their desire is not just to know where babies come from, but more sweeping, profound, and existential. In the second number, "All That's Known," the girls' male counterparts are reciting Latin in an oppressive classroom, where adults insist that the only real knowledge is found in old books. But our young hero Melchoir sees the hypocrisy of their doctrine, his gloriously optimistic ballad soaring over the drone of ancient language: "I know there's so much more to find / just in looking through myself and not at them."

Hunger is the driving force of this show, extending from the first few scenes to the tragic conclusion. The language the teenage characters use to describe their desire is equally heightened whether they are singing about their intellectual lives or the pleasure of masturbation. And although there is sex onstage, both described and performed, these young people are not singing only, or even primarily, about sex. The adults in their lives who claim to think that it's all about lust are missing the point. These songs are about a hunger for transgression, including and beyond the carnal: enlightenment, unity, freedom. These are desires that the repressive adult regime has every reason to fear.

Unlike the shows in the musical theater pantheon that Wolf (Stacy, not the other one) shows us how to read subversively, my three bucket-list musicals explicitly stage queer desire. *Rent* gives us Joanne and Maureen, Angel and Tom, "faggots, lezzies, dykes, cross-dressers too." *Spring Awakening* has teenage boys lusting after their classmates in the shower. *Hedwig*, of course, has Hedwig. As queer desire is more explicitly staged, so too is the devastation wrought by such desire. Yet even in this devastation, when the protagonist loses everything and is brought, often literally, to their knees, in all three shows we get a transcendent ending that lifts up into joy and communion. These endings perform the risks and rewards of full-throated, multivalent, boundary-crossing desire.

Listening now, I hear in the endings of these three musicals a different final thesis than in traditional narrative, where the continued existence of desire is incompatible with a happy ending. Yes, all three end with soaring, unifying finales—"Finale B," "The Song of Purple Summer," and "Midnight Radio," respectively. But immediately before that final song, each has what might be called an "I *still* wish" song that performs the often literal co-existence of desire and death. The penultimate position it occupies in the narrative is a neat mirror of the traditional "I wish" position, a beautifully queer almost-ending.

In *Hedwig*, it's "Wicked Little Town," the pop ballad that Hedwig once sang to Tommy, sung back to her by him as a healing offering after she has violently destroyed her physical and creative self. As both roles are played by the same actor, we can see before our eyes the co-existence of death and desire in one body. In *Rent*, Roger must perform a literal embrace of a fused desire and death as he sings his "one great song" to a dying Mimi ("Your Eyes"). And in *Spring Awakening*, Melchoir kneels in a graveyard, beginning a heartbroken and defeated reprise of his "I wish" song, "All That's Known." As he sings, the ghosts of his lost friends appear, whispering their love, support, and hope, reminding him of what he believes, transforming his song into a liberating re-commitment to living fully, without fear, in pursuit of truth and freedom. Melchoir's eleventh hour re-assertion of desire affirms for us that to continue to reach out, through longing, through loss, to "trust your own true mind," is the most heroic act—an embrace of hope in the face of the world's darkness that gifts us an authentically complex, fully felt happy ending.

These endings give us desire and death, together. We watch characters—no longer coded—who take big risks on outsize, out-of-bounds desire, who encounter death and survive. Not every character in these narratives lives, but by giving us the hopeful unification of desire and death in the text rather than the subtext, these musicals offer extraordinary opportunities for audiences to practice queer survival.

In the W-O-L-F days, I was also for a time obsessed with "The

Three Little Pigs"—yes, on a Disney read-along record. Two of the pig brothers were lazy and idle; they built their houses out of straw and twigs, respectively, in order to have the time to play the flute and violin and dance around the meadow without pants on. The third pig, who wears overalls and has a deeper voice, unlike the squeaky sopranos of his brothers, isn't afraid of hard work, "You can play and laugh and fiddle, don't think you can make me sore. I'll be safe and you'll be sorry when the wolf comes to your door." And indeed, the pants-less little pigs *are* sorry, when the Big Bad Wolf huffs and puffs and blows their houses in. I shudder to think of their fate if they hadn't had a brother with a brick house to run to.

These are the warning tales about nonconformity—that is, queerness—that demonstrate the misguided and destructive wish for pleasure. Wanting to laugh, to play, to make music, to run outside, to bask in the hedonism of freedom—these impulses put you in danger, make you vulnerable to ruin. Stay good, stay vigilant, stay straight or the darkness will destroy everything you own, everything you have built, even your own body. It will blow down the walls that keep you safe, it will demolish your livelihood, it will stop at nothing, it will consume you.

If my childhood terror of the W-O-L-F was a terror at the force of my own desire, and how vulnerable it made me, and if, by listening and re-listening, I was practicing a critical encounter with fused desire and terror, an encounter necessary to step fully into the queerness I was not yet ready to sing—then it seems clearer why I stubbornly mis-remembered the ending of *Peter and The Wolf,* recalling the Duck's tragic fate rather than Peter's triumphant capture of the Wolf, or even the Disney-approved eleventh-hour Duck reprieve.

In the original piece of music and narration, we have the Wolf as villain, Peter as hero, and the Duck as horrifying semi-casualty, trapped forever inside the carnivore. In this ending, the peril represented by the Wolf has been captured and contained, so the Boy is free to roam where he pleases. This is a happy ending, but only for Boys. For Ducks, or a little girl whose first word was "duck," the ending is not a happy one. She is somehow both forgotten and punished, trapped in the belly of peril—contained forever in a cage of caged Wolf. The lesson: If I abandon care, if I get too close to that hungry mouth, I will be consumed. And when the Boy cleverly traps the Wolf and puts it in a cage, I, too, will go to the cage. Because I failed to avoid the danger, I will be punished as if I am part of it. As if I, too, am dangerous.

It is here that Disney intervenes, glossily but imperfectly papering over this conclusion—the Duck comes out from her hiding place, and all is well! But there is a cost to her survival, a cost not incurred by the Boy, who is still free to roam, nor by the wily Cat nor the swift Bird (both gendered male in the Disney version) who assist the Boy in his feat of capture. For the Duck, however, even in the happy(er) version, there is just one way to avoid destruction: she can hide. She emerges only in the final moment, tentative and shaken. And of course, Prokofiev's original music lurks under this amendment, militant and grim.

I might have listened over and over again hoping I would hear something different. Couldn't the Duck, like Red Riding Hood's grandmother, slice her way out? Or what if, this time, from her hiding place, she steps into a more active role, providing some essential part of the Wolf-capture-plan?

This de-centered kind of listening strikes me as essentially queer—an out-of-bounds noticing, attending to the edges of the narrative, imagining alternatives. It's clear that I wasn't especially interested in Peter's story of capturing the Wolf, or in pigs who live in brick houses; I was listening to the story in the margins, learning the lessons of the sidekick, the best friend, the funny co-worker, the nosy neighbor—all classic queer character tropes. I am there, I am determined to be there, but I have to stretch to find me. It takes work.

Really, the queerest reading of *Peter and the Wolf* would probably be to empathize with the Wolf, to imagine a version of the story where the Wolf is tamed with love or song and becomes friends with the others, frolicking together in the forest—or, even better, where there is an alliance between Duck and Wolf and they live happily ever after together even as it looks to the rest of the world like they are in a cage.

At the time I didn't have the imaginative fortitude for that kind of queer reading. The Wolf is meant to be terrifying, and I was, as I was meant to be, terrified. W-O-L-F.

But I was interested in that terror. It was a big feeling. I turned towards it, instead of away. I wanted to feel a feeling with that *size*, again and again. I re-listened to *Peter and The Wolf* because the cosmic terror dwarfed the happy endings on the rest of my Disney read-along records, and feeling something huge made me feel alive, made me feel most like myself.

As I moved from high school to college to that apartment in the Meat Packing district, as I watched and loved *Rent* and *Hedwig* and *Spring Awakening*, I had a series of male suitors and a healthy dose of heartbreak. In those years, though Liza and I shared an intimacy far beyond what I shared with any boyfriend, we never kissed. At least as far as I remember, we stayed within the bounds of the prescribed narrative. We were friends.

I've always thought this was because I didn't understand how I felt about her at the time, that it became clear to me only later. But then, while working on this essay, I find a stack of paper stashed in a dresser drawer at my parents' house. It's a two-inch thick print-out of emails from the first six weeks I ever had email—like, ever. I suppose I didn't quite trust the medium. The emails are all between me and Liza. I was still in high school, she'd gone off to college, and they read just like the correspondence of every other young couple that's been separated in this way. Promises to stay true forever, earnest over-statements of affection, ardently possessive language.

Reading these, I'm freed from the burden of imagining that I didn't understand my desire. It is evident that I wanted what I wanted with a startling power. And what I wanted was to be as near to Liza as possible. To experience the world with her, through her, to become what she saw in me, to make and remake each other.

I can also see that, like a million heartsick letter-writers before me, I was small in the shadow of my big feelings. My submission to this overwhelming radiance of Liza felt both wrong and good. The combination of shame and pleasure was confusing; I thought no one would understand. I believed, as I'd been taught by so many stories, that I could only survive by concealing the size of what I felt—but I was also tempted to see what I could get away with. I would slide her name into conversation, casual as any other noun. Was she like a ghost that only I could see? Or would everyone around me feel the blaze of her name scorching its way through a forest of ordinary words?

They did not. I learned that I could hide in plain sight.

I didn't proclaim my wish.

As a child, as a teen, as a young adult, I was terrified by what

I sensed was at the door: the force of my own keen appetite, the dark carnivore in my forest. I was terrified—but I was also curious. I returned over and over to the site of terror. I learned that it wouldn't kill me. I searched for another narrative—one that didn't start with singing "I wish" and end with "happily ever after." I understood that the old familiar story wasn't *my* story. If indeed it is anyone's story, which I'm not totally sure that it is, but *if* it is, it's a very straight story. In a straight story, a queer protagonist can't proclaim her wish. She can't be heroic in her attempt to achieve it. She doesn't get a happy ending. And I *want* a happy ending. Which means wanting a different story.

Last week it seemed like everyone in my social media feed was posting a video of M.J. Rodriguez and George Salazar on late-night TV singing the duet "Suddenly Seymour" from *Little Shop of Horrors*. As I write this, the two are starring in director Mike Donahue's production of the cult musical at Pasadena Playhouse, which takes the (radical, according to most media coverage) route of portraying the show's Skid Row denizens with total truth and heart. The cast is mostly actors of color; the leading man Seymour is played by Salazar, a gay Filipino/Ecuadorian man, the leading lady Audrey by Rodriguez, an African-American/Puerto-Rican transgender woman.

It is a stunning and completely moving performance, notable not only for its piercing sincerity and unadorned artistry, but also because the song seems to have been waiting since 1982 for these two to come along and sing it. Ah, the song is saying, *now* I can reveal the size of my truth to you. This song where Seymour tells Audrey "you don't need no makeup, don't have to pretend," where Audrey lights up with the revelation that "I can learn how to be more, the girl that's inside me!," where the soaring duet's climax is the now heart-rending lyric "with sweet understanding" repeated four times in a row.

Little Shop has always been a show that defied genre, and perhaps its conclusion—bloody death and campy fun, threatening and joyful all at once—has always been queer. But in this version, where the queerness is lifted out of the coded and subversive, it feels finally fulfilled.

"Suddenly Seymour" is not *Little Shop*'s "I wish" song. The show does have a great one though—the alarmingly catchy 60's pop-rock "Skid Row." I wish I could hear Rodriguez and Salazar sing it. But that's one thing about live theater—if you're not in the room where it happens, you might just miss it forever. I can imagine it, though. I can imagine just how it would feel hearing those two sing the familiar lyrics—about being poor all your life, about scrubbing rich people's bathrooms and then going home to a neighborhood where the cabs won't stop, about never being valued or respected, and longing, longing to get out.

My eyes fill up just thinking about them singing it. And maybe that's good enough. We've long been queering "Skid Row," and every other "I Wish" song—just by listening. If you don't believe me, try it. As an experiment, put on the original cast recording of *Little Shop*—or, if by the time you're reading this, you actually can listen to the Rodriguez/Salazar version, please do. We're living in the Spotify age, so I know, if you have your phone nearby, you can do this in a few taps.

Do you have it on?

I put in my earbuds, tap play, breathe into the opening piano notes. The feeling of relief is immediate. As the snare drops in, a smile creeps over my face, I can feel my toes and my head start to bob. As the harmony swells, as the chorus drives, I feel myself expand. As they sing, I rehearse: my desire, my self, larger, larger, larger, sometimes getting almost to full-size before the song ends.

The Hero Gotham Deserves

Yes, it is me. Shui Ta and Shen Teh, I am both of them.
Your original order
To be good while yet surviving
Split me like lightning into two people. I
Cannot tell what occurred: goodness to others
And to myself could not both be achieved.

– *Good Person of Szechwan*, Bertolt Brecht

As a baby, one of my favorite books was called *Babies*. *Babies* was a large board book showing small children of various hues eating, sleeping, bathing, and playing in wonderful illustrations by Gyo Fujikawa (who was ahead of her time on the "various hues" thing). According to my mother, my favorite page was the one with the "naughty" babies who were sticking their fingers in the jam jar, fighting over a toy, and in a meta move, tearing pages out of a book. Whenever we got to that page, I would wag my finger at the bad babies, enthusiastically scolding "No, no, no!"

I don't remember doing this—don't remember pointing to the shelf to request the book, or eagerly flipping the heavy pages to reach the naughty page. But based on what I know about myself as an adult, it feels right. I still appreciate storytelling that makes it clear which are the naughty characters and which are the good ones. Now, as then, I like to know which page *I'm* on—always with the desire to establish that I am *not* on the naughty page. A clear split—naughty versus nice—makes it easier to locate myself. It also, as baby-me knew, makes the reading of the naughty page much more pleasurable. If you are sure that you, personally, are a good baby, it's great fun to shake your finger at those with jam all over their faces.

A split puts things in their place. If we don't consign "goodness" to one page and "naughtiness" to another, we're forced to consider the instability of our own location. Ambiguity and complexity, not to mention integration or intersectionality, are risky. By leaving space, by deliberately crossing wires, we invite disorder—even chaos.

The adult, or adult-ish, equivalent of the *Babies* book is a good action movie, particularly of the superhero variety. These films typically give us a crystal clear delineation of right and wrong, so that we can shake our finger at the villain and cheer for the hero. It is so clear who is bad and who is good that, in spite of the very loud sound effects, I find them almost soothing to watch.

Many great superhero stories are structured on a double split— there is the good/bad split of hero/villain, and then there is the split within each character—Peter Parker/Spiderman, Green Goblin/Norman Osborne; Clark Kent/Superman, Lex Luthor-as-philanthropist-and-industrialist/Lex Luthor-as-diabolical-genius. This internal split may begin as a practical matter—the "regular person" identity is intended to disguise the super-identity, hypothetically allowing the hero to live undetected in ordinary society—but it quickly becomes an obstacle. A hero's internal battle is often just as central to super-story-lines as his battle with a villain, and we become equally as invested in rooting for the hero to become heroic as we do in rooting for him (yes, traditionally him) to defeat the villain once he does.

Batman has a particularly intense internal split. Living in Gotham City as billionaire playboy Bruce Wayne, the character swings between whole-hearted embrace of his crime-fighting bat-identity and misanthropic seclusion. My introduction to this character came in the form of Christopher Nolan's movie trilogy—*Batman Begins, The Dark Knight*, and *The Dark Knight Rises*—which, as actors I've directed can tell you, are frequent points of reference in my rehearsal process. Though the three constitute a near-perfect film triumvirate, full of great performances, complex characterizations, and metaphors that become more resonant over time, it is *The Dark Knight* that I keep coming back to. As the middle of the trilogy, it can afford a dark ambiguity not possible in parts one and three.

When the film begins, Bruce Wayne longs to retire his bat persona and live a normal life with the woman he loves. His hopes are pinned on Gotham's new District Attorney, Harvey Dent, who seems capable of transforming the city so drastically that it will no longer need Batman. Towards this end, Dent and soon-to-be-named Police Commissioner Gordon partner with

Batman to rid Gotham of organized crime. It turns out, though, that what they are up against is the antithesis of "organized." Instead it is the poster-child of *dis*organization: The Joker, portrayed by Heath Ledger with anarchic intensity. Director Christopher Nolan said the film was inspired in large part by the 1940 comic that introduced the Joker, in which "there was this fascinating idea that Batman's presence in Gotham actually attracts criminals to Gotham, attracts lunacy." And indeed *The Dark Knight* gives us a curious symbiosis between Christian Bale's stoic, dark hero and Ledger's brightly incendiary villain.

Batman initially follows the classic rules of the villain/hero battle, in which the former wants to destroy the world and the latter wants to save it. At times The Joker seems to be playing along. Several times he declares that the two are locked in "a battle for the soul of Gotham city"—a phrase that would be oft-repeated by critics to describe the film—but mostly The Joker refuses to have a motive, an intention, or a destination. He foils every showdown by sending our hero running away to avert some other, worse catastrophe that he has set in motion. The Joker stands still while Batman, and the city, run frantically around him. Refusing to conform to the supervillain blueprint, the Joker doesn't want power and he doesn't want money (in fact, when he gets a giant pile of it, he pointedly sets it on fire). He doesn't want to destroy the world, or to dominate it. He wants to destabilize, to unhinge, to reverse. He reveals the ways that the world is irrational and unpredictable, conforming, like him, to only one law: chaos. "You have these rules. And you think they'll save you," the Joker helpfully explains to Batman in one of the film's most disturbing scenes, an interrogation where Batman becomes increasingly enraged and violent as the Joker becomes calmer and more delighted, "The only sensible way to live in this world is without rules." Soon after The Joker provokes the dark side of the Dark Knight, he visits the "white knight" District Attorney in the hospital. DA Dent, distraught over his physical disfigurement and the death of his fiancée, needs only a nudge to transform into Two-Face, the chance-obsessed villain who uses a coin flip to determine whether to turn his brand of vigilante justice on small children—or not.

What is the gravitational pull of this murky middle film on a girl who liked to know the good babies from the bad babies? I must admit, I do like that chaos is the villain here. Although its anarchic mayhem is thrilling (if terrifying), the film is clearly painting disorder as bad and order as good. Unlike a classic villain, the Joker has no tidy internal split. Even his origin story is chaotic—he makes up a new one every time he gets the chance, inventing some fresh trauma to explain his haunting grimace. And when he philosophizes to Dent, "You know the thing about chaos? It's *fair!,*" we understand that this is both true and wrong. The Joker is promoting his own brand of what might be called "vigilante chaos"—as a rational response and even remedy for the organized, state-sanctioned violence of governments and systems.

In *The Dark Knight*'s final scene between Batman and the Joker, the world is turned upside down—literally. Batman has captured the Joker, and has him hanging by his feet off a skyscraper—but the camera slowly tilts to show the Joker's face right-side up, the now-inverted city dropping eerily behind him. He appears to have been defeated and captured, but the Joker is laughing and in control. The movie goes on to conclude with Batman defeating Two-Face and taking the blame for his murders, fleeing into the night, as, according to Commissioner Gordon, "the hero Gotham deserves." Gordon chooses an illusion for the people of Gotham—the fantasy of reason over the reality of madness, the sham protection of a corrupt system of law and order over the reality of its rot. The pretense that Batman is behind the murders actually committed by Two-Face preserves the myth of the hero, albeit with a twist. The people of Gotham have Harvey Dent as their hero and Batman as their villain, and we, the audience, have it the other way around. Either way, the cover-up slices the complex and messy truth into a cleanly split lie.

This lie will preserve our (both the audience's and Gotham's) belief in a moral universe, which is the only thing keeping us from sliding into chaos. This idea of good and evil is more important than who is good and who is evil. The split is an organizational strategy for surviving in a terrifyingly complex world. In this sense, I read the ending of *The Dark Knight* as a "happy ending"—an ending that, while cynical about the costs of heroism, believes in goodness and altruism, an ending that offers a way to live forward with a sense of meaning and hope.

This seems right, but there's a catch, in superhero movies especially. If our "happy ending" preserves the split, then it preserves not only the heroic force, but also the villainous one. If the happy ending is a triumph for the hero, it's also an invitation to the next villain. Thus splitting as an organizational strategy for achieving safety ultimately ensures our peril—just as this kind of "happy ending" ensures a sequel—by refusing to integrate the existence of destructive forces into its portrait of a just world.

But what if the narrative, instead, had a chaotic ending? Would that be an unhappy ending? One of my favorite stories *does* end this way—sort of. That story, Bertolt Brecht's 1941 play *The Good Person of Szechwan*, is set in a metropolis very much like Gotham—a dark city, where the wealthy eat their fill with their feet on the necks of the poor. As the play begins, three Gods have descended to earth to assess the moral state of humanity; they have decreed that "the world can go on as it is if we find enough good people." Upon arrival in Szechwan, they quickly identify Shen Teh, a prostitute with a heart of gold, as a perfect specimen of goodness. When she protests ("I am by no means sure that I am good. I should certainly like to be, but how am I to pay the rent?"), they gift her with a bag of gold and continue on their travels, seeking good people in other cities. Shen Teh eagerly invests her new fortune in a small tobacco shop, dreaming of making a respectable living and providing charity to her neighbors. Yet she soon finds herself overrun by Szechwan's desperate and ruthless citizens, who take advantage of her generosity and nearly ruin her. Distressing consequences

THERE MUST BE HAPPY ENDINGS

result from her good deeds; her attempts to behave morally lead to impossible ethical dilemmas. The pure-hearted Shen Teh, in the photo-negative of the superhero trope, dons a costume and a mask not in order to protect the people of Szechwan but in order to protect herself *from* them. Shen Teh's alter-ego, her "cousin" Shui Ta, saves her business and her reputation by underpaying contractors and turning street kids over to the police. Eventually, Shui Ta makes a fortune selling ruinous drugs to the community he (as she) previously nurtured. "Something is wrong with this world of yours," Shen Teh rails at the Gods when they finally return to Szechwan, "Why is wickedness so rewarded, and why is so much suffering reserved for the good?"

The end of the play has the Gods ascend serenely back to heaven "on a pink cloud," leaving Shen Teh screaming after them, at the mercy of the world they have decidedly *not* fixed. It is a chaotic, disorderly ending—which the text cheerfully admits in a brief epilogue, wherein a player steps forward to explain that "nothing's been arranged" for the ending of the play, and asks the audience for their opinion:

> *"There's only one solution that we know*
> *That you should now consider as you go*
> *What sort of measures you would recommend*
> *To help good people to a happy end."*

I've always loved this epilogue—so much that I took from it the title of this book. Without the epilogue, *Good Person's* chaotic ending, like the orderly ending of *Dark Knight,* leaves us stuck in a co-dependent cycle of heroism and villainy. However, the coda eloquently shifts the framing of the problem from one of personal complexity (whether it is permissible or even possible for our hero to be both Shen Teh and Shui Ta) to one of systemic injustice. This double ending doesn't condemn the complex individual for her efforts to survive in the horrifying world. Rather, it seeks to lay bare the problem of the horrifying world—that it splits us from ourselves. It first demonstrates the hopeless situation, and then, through the grace of the coda, gestures towards the hopeful possibility of a remedy. By saying "Sorry that the ending is so unsatisfying. We don't know what else to do. Do you?," the epilogue doesn't provide an alternative ending so much as a critique of the ending—of both the conclusion of the play, and of classic narrative structure.

The *Good Person* epilogue makes the ending hopeful because it proposes an alternative to the traditional resolution and its recommitment to the split, to the triumph of totalizing order over terrifying chaos. In it we glimpse the possibility that the remedy for an unjust system is in the hands of complex individuals—us—neither bad nor good, but whole and unconstrained by narrative conventions. A happy ending might yet be found, but not within the constraints of a story whose structure echoes the structure of an unjust system.

When I directed *Good Person*, my production—no surprise here—had a comic-book-noir aesthetic inspired in part by *The*

Dark Knight. I badly wanted the audience, in the end, to feel the lift and breath that I feel in the epilogue, to feel transformed and enlivened by the twinned upending and embrace of the "happy" ending. I wanted it to be one of Jill Dolan's "utopian performatives": the kind of theater-going experience that provides a vivid feeling of beauty and togetherness, an experience of watching that gifts spectators with a glimpse of a potential new social reality. This kind of experience, Dolan writes, and I fervently agree, can sustain us in our daily lives as we labor to shape the world in the image of the beloved community glimpsed during performance.

But, watching, I could feel that the production did not achieve this.

And, in fact, in spite of my conviction that *Good Person* is perfectly positioned to gift us the experience of a utopian performative, I haven't yet seen it happen. As an avid *Good Person* fan girl, I've seen what I would characterize as two important contemporary American productions of the play: The Foundry Theatre's cheeky 2013 version at La MaMa helmed by one of our most utopian directors, Lear deBessonet, with Taylor Mac in the title role, and more recently Eric Ting's intense, emotionally grounded 2019 production at California Shakespeare Theater's gorgeous outdoor amphitheater. The former was fast and loose and warm-hearted, the latter, archly deliberate, blisteringly funny, and wrenching. In both cases, I entered the theater with great anticipation and enthusiasm, and left feeling full, as if

I had been at a long dinner party (the play runs nearly three hours) with serious, sparklingly smart guests whose "banter" required my deep intellectual investment. While both productions offered many pleasures—provocative questions, deep belly laughs, good music, great performances—they did not send me out of the theater lifted up with the restorative glow that comes from having had the chance, for a few brief hours, to practice utopian social relations in the temporary community of an audience.

I wonder if this is because a utopian performative must allow for transformation—of the world, of individual human beings, of our felt sense of community—*within* the narrative structure. Since *Good Person* gestures beyond the narrative for this hope, does it break the container that we need for this kind of transformative experience?

I ordered a used copy of *Babies* on Amazon, and it turns out that the book is not actually about good babies and bad babies. It is, rather, about the category of "babies." It clearly makes a case for baby complexity—individual babies are, at different times, naughty and angelic, sleepy and hungry, happy and sad. In fact, the page after the "naughty" babies shows the very same babies as "little angels"—cradling the book lovingly, staring wistfully at the unopened jam jar. *The same babies!* The book does *not* make the case that some babies are bad while other babies are good—that was an idea that I, a baby myself, imported. There aren't any adults in the book; no babies are being rewarded or punished for their behavior. They are simply their full baby selves. It offers a well-balanced baby ecosystem, complex *and* orderly. This seems like an ideal book for me, lover of the split, to have read over and over, a text that might have influenced me in the direction of embracing my internal complexity.

And yet, it did not.

"Megan!" I scold myself, "It's so obvious: the split is *bad* and complexity is *good*!"

Classic. Even in my attempt to transcend the split, I can create a split.

Had I, at age one or two, already internalized this split so deeply that I was able to read it into a text that attempted to resist it? Who taught me to love wagging my finger at the naughty page? How did I learn that naughty babies get finger wagging, while angelic babies get cuddles and love? What happened to convince me that I could be either one thing or the other? And how do I now, presumably in the middle movie of the trilogy of my life, allow myself the murkiness that wasn't possible in the beginning?

Looking at the delighted, jam-covered baby on the naughty page of my new-to-me copy, it occurs to me that it would be possible to read the book as being about what to *do*, rather than who to *be*. In that case, the utility of the book is not in the pleasure of scolding ("No, no, no!"), which is a way of declaring myself distinct from and superior to other babies; nor is it in the searching for an acceptable location for myself on the "good baby" page, which is a maneuver for erasing or denying my internal complexity. Rather, I can safely experiment with affinity for the jam-covered baby or the jam-holding baby, noting the possible consequences of their actions. My essential question as a reader shifts from "Am I good or am I bad?" to "How can I recognize myself in those who act both rightly and wrongly?" My reading becomes enlivening rather than defensive.

Brecht's coda, too, is about what to *do*—it is not interested in judging good and bad, but in how we might change the world around us. The problems of the play, it says, cannot honestly be resolved until we tackle the problems of the world. What action can we take?

Little plot twist about the *Good Person* epilogue, though: it is not, exclusively, Brecht's ending. Harold Bloom begins his introduction to a volume of analysis on the playwright's work by acknowledging that "Brecht" is now known to be less an author's name than a brand name (an aptly insulting desig-nation for a writer who spent so much time railing against Capitalism). It's widely acknowledged that large portions of Brecht's major plays were written with, and in some cases by, a group of women with whom he was romantically and artistically entangled. Margarete Steffin and Ruth Berlau were collabora-tors on, if not majority authors of, *The Good Person of Szechwan*.

This gives us an enraging and intriguing authorial split—a secret alter-ego behind the mask of the heroic playwright.

Some critics have suggested the play as a dialectic, a conversation between its female authors and its male one. In the realm of intellect, this makes sense. In the realm of reality—where Brecht, like Shui Ta, appropriated and profited from the perspective, skill and labor of his unacknowledged female collaborators—it is harder to stomach. Brecht did not completely erase these women—on some publications, they are listed alongside composers as "collaborators"—but they were (and are) not included on the covers of the books, on the posters for the plays, in his theoretical writings, or in the larger cultural conversation about "Brecht's" work. Their ending—which, from here, cannot be said to be happy—demonstrates what is lost, and who it costs, when complexity is denied in service of an over-determined desire for heroic figures.

Throughout my relationship with this text, I've felt my deep love for its ending in conflict with the authorial problems. "I love this ending" versus "This ending was not created fairly." But maybe this is just another split. Can I allow the complexities of authorship to deepen my love, rather than undermine it? Rather than de-legitimize the work, can the split authorship amplify my reading of the split central character? Can the reality of the text's multiple authors make the text's offer to the audience—to become co-authors of the ending—weightier and more authentic? Yes, I think so.

"Brecht"'s play insists on an unresolvable binary split between good and bad that is also a split between woman and man, pleasure and business, passion and career, intuition and intellect. But "Brecht"'s epilogue tells a different story. It acknowledges that the ending is unsatisfying, that both the world of the play and the form of the narrative, as constructed, preclude justice. It expresses its longing for something better. It reiterates the unresolvable questions and lovingly, hopefully turns them over to the audience. Because the *Good Person* epilogue exists outside of the narrative (split) world, it offers the possibility that we could choose to strive together for something more just, a world that would allow for complexity and perhaps even integration, a world not reliant on and reinforcing of the split.

Reading this ending while holding the complex truth of its authorship makes *Good Person*'s coda expansively polyvalent—as in, holding more than two possible meanings, and also "effective against more than one toxin, microorganism, or antigen," language that sounds like it's straight out of a superhero film. The polyvalence of the *Good Person* epilogue might counteract the existential terror we feel at the play's chaotic conclusion, might counteract my own censure of that terror, might even counteract the lack of a utopian audience experience. I'm not entirely sure it can be effective against the powerful lingering effects of one particular reading of the *Babies* book—but you know, there's still time.

As I reach the end of this essay, I can feel myself desperately wanting an ordered ending, some kind of action that will help you, and me, make meaning from the chaos, the kind of ending that, when you read it aloud, produces a satisfying and memorable exhale following the last period.

So what I'm wondering is, does this happy ending—and does the experience of utopian possibility—have to come by way of an illusory order, a tidy lie to mask the chaotic truth? Do we have to vanquish the terrifying realities of injustice and chaos from our finale? Or can we find hope in the reach for an ending that acknowledges both order and chance, grace and terror? Can such a finish ever really *feel* finished? I'm not sure. But I am curious—curious enough to risk my own success, my own goodness, to investigate. What if we imagine this ending allows the tension between the split parts to continue, instead of resolving it? Could we imagine this ending admits, "yes, I am both of them, I am all of them"? And then maybe it stands there, being both and all, breathing, looking out at you, as the house lights slowly, slowly come up.

A Lamp, A Bridge, A Ship

I heard once that the Dalai Lama starts every day with the same prayer. A few lines of it persistently return to me, the way prayers and poems do: in pieces, imperfectly remembered, arriving unbidden, departing just as suddenly. "Let me be a lamp in the darkness, a bridge for those with rivers to cross, a ship for those with oceans to cross."

These lines come to me as I zip up my boots, swing my backpack on, scrape the ice off the windshield. They arrive as I change lanes, as I look for parking, as I step into the darkened pre-tech theater and swing my backpack down again. The lighting and sound designers are typing behind consoles, speaking into headsets. Young people with tools clinking on their belts adjust things in the ceiling and the floor and the walls. There is painting, drilling, sweeping; with a moment of warning ("Going dark!" "Sound in the house!"), light and sound charge across the space.

Every time, I'm humbled by the number of people who work together to make a play.

I want to guide them with kindness and grace. I want to speak to the work ahead with clarity and energy. I want to move with the conviction that this story matters, to ensure that everyone in the room feels welcomed and inspired and part of something. I know that the tone of my voice or the tilt of my head has the power to shift everyone's energy, for better or for worse.

It's just a play, of course. But almost every time, it happens:

The play is about the end of a marriage. One of the actors is in the process of ending their marriage.

The play is about an abused woman trying to escape her marriage and save her child. One of the actors has the same story in their family; their mother was that mother, and ran to save them.

The play is about the aftermath of a suicide. Any number of the actors have recently lost someone in that way.

The play includes a miscarriage. One of the actors has recently had a miscarriage, although she won't speak about it in the rehearsal room. Only I know.

So, from first rehearsal to opening night, I need to be able to hold the space for this work to be catharsis and healing, for it to be both craft and truth, for it to go far enough but not too far. I have to breathe into a deep place of compassion, of complete attention, and also hold the frame. They are relying on me for this. Without the frame of task—in the next two hours, we have to perfect this card-playing sequence in the second act—we would spiral into the raw space of unbounded feeling. The structure of task makes the work possible; the compassionate container keeps it safe.

It's a tender kind of intuition that tells me when to stop the rehearsal and gather in a cross-legged circle on the floor. Equally tender is the instinct for when I must push us forward. Sometimes the circle has opened up some space for exploration; doing the scene again afterwards will be breathtaking. Sometimes the circle has exposed something raw and tender, something that needs time to gestate; the right thing to do is to move onto a different scene, or even end the rehearsal. Early in my career, I used to consult the room in moments like this, "what do you want to do now?" Occasionally I still do, but I've come to understand that part of my job is to know more than they do about what will be best for the group in these moments.

In fact, moving with the confidence that I know how to take care of the group, that I can keep them safe, that I am closely listening and watching, is essential. If doubt creeps into the room about whether or not I can firmly hold this container, then suddenly the work becomes much harder, and more dangerous, for all of us.

There are some things I remember learning how to do, that I still do exactly the same way, just as I was taught. How to cut an avocado—halving it lengthwise, then striking the edge of a large knife into the exposed seed to lift it out—which my brother learned in a cooking class and then passed on to me. How to beat an egg into hot soup without curdling it—by stirring a cup of hot broth slowly, by teaspoonfuls, into the small bowl with the beaten egg—learned at a young age from my mother since it was a key step in Armenian-style chicken soup, which I ate whenever I was ill. How to properly make a bed—fold the bedspread down, place the pillows slightly overlapping it, and then fold the bedspread neatly up and over the pillows so it outlines their shape—drilled into me by my grandmother during summers at the beach, where one of our morning chores was to make up the twin beds that she and my grandfather slept in.

I don't remember, though, anyone teaching me how to direct a play. I learned pieces from various places—from my dad, from Peter Brook's *The Empty Space*, and from Lowry Marshall, the college acting teacher who was the first person to suggest I might be a director and who gave me a cryptic but useful piece of theatrical advice I've never forgotten: "God hates transitions" (best said in Lowry's North Carolina drawl).

Perhaps as a result, in the absence of rules, I developed a kind of magical thinking about directing. I had to feel a certain way, I had to breathe a certain way, I had to wait for the pieces to fit just so. There was no system, no method. There were only experiments that could be tried, results that could be observed, feelings that could be felt.

When I was in college and in my early years in the professional world, I'd never read a book about directing written by a female director. There were books on acting by Stella Adler and Uta Hagen, and Viola Spolin's wonderful book on improvisation, but these didn't speak to the questions I didn't even know then that I had—how to lead a process, how to hold a generative container with grace and authority. By the time I was in grad school, a few of Anne Bogart's books were available and I read them voraciously. I liked that she had written them and I liked how they felt in my hand—compact, smooth, poetic.

One particular idea of hers stuck in my mind: that the director is the person who can tolerate uncertainty the longest of anyone else in the room. I always remembered this, and I shaped my idea of myself as a director in its image—cultivating a grounded, calm demeanor and a gentle energy, practicing holding space for whatever might emerge.

When I went back to Bogart's books while writing this essay, to find the line I'd been quoting, I found that Bogart herself was quoting someone else—the playwright Charles Mee. Mee's definition of a director, Bogart writes, is "the person in the room who can maintain the anxiety of possibility and uncertainty the longest." It turns out that she was using Mee's concept as a foil, a way of opening up her own focus on precision, on articulation.

More often, in contrast, Bogart writes of the director's role in perpetrating "the necessary cruelty of decision." Art, she says, is violent because it makes choices:

> *To be decisive is violent.... To place a chair at a particu-*
> *lar angle on the stage destroys every other possible choice,*
> *every other option. When an actor achieves a spontaneous,*
> *intuitive, or passionate moment in rehearsal, the direc-*
> *tor utters the fateful words 'keep it,' eliminating all other*
> *potential solutions....But, deep down, the actor also knows*
> *that improvisation is not yet art. Only when something*
> *has been decided can the work really begin.*

I love both Bogart's and Mee's way of describing the work of directing. It strikes me, though, that for all these years I'd held onto the part about possibility and uncertainty, while allowing violence and cruelty to lapse out of sight. In my field of vision: the part of my job that was open, spacious. Just outside of it: the part that was ruthless.

Playwright Quiara Alegria Hudes gave a talk at the Association of Theatre in Higher Education, later reprinted in *American Theatre Magazine,* called "The High Tide of Heartbreak," in which she asked "Has theatre wounded me as much as or more than it's healed me?" Hudes talked about the suffering she'd experienced over the course of her career, the harm that the toxins of white supremacy and patriarchy were able to do to her through the workings of the American theater, even as an artist seemingly anointed by the establishment, who'd been awarded both the Tony and the Pulitzer before the age of 40. She talked about being both deeply proud of her work and deeply injured by it, and wondered if the work was worth the wound. She reflected on the agonizing, loving labor of crafting working class Puerto Rican characters inspired by her family, and wondered if putting them onstage for a majority white audience was the equivalent of cultural tourism, rendering their culture exotic and their poverty monstrous. She wondered if she had, in her quest to honor them, in fact insulted her family and her community by putting their truth onstage in such a context. She asked, "Is honesty, which I strive for, also a form of violence?"

Reading, I felt a stomach-sinking wave of recognition. Hudes said publicly what I'd heard whispered in lobbies and bars and the back row of conference sessions for years—what I'd thought myself so many times—that the cost of making theater is too high to justify the benefit. These whispers are most often from those of us—like me, like Hudes—who are most vulnerable to the harm of theater-making precisely because we are most in need of its benefits. Artists who are female, of color, or queer, or immigrants, who are Deaf or autistic or use a wheelchair, who come from poverty, who don't live in a major city and didn't go to a fancy school, who are fat, who identify outside of the gender binary—we long for images that include us, we are hungry for spaces of empathy and imagination, we yearn for a seat at the table, to see that our stories belong here too.

But the balance had tipped for Hudes: the harm outweighed the good. She was stepping away.

I have not stepped away; this is still what I do. I want to insist that it is possible to make truthful *and* ethical performance, theater that does no damage to human minds and bodies in service of aesthetic aims. I am also mindful of what I learned and then forgot and then relearned from Anne Bogart—that violence is necessary to make art. But there's a critical distinction between violence and harm. Violence is strong, powerful, forceful. It can be destructive, yes—but it can just as easily be generative. A roadblock can be exploded to allow free passage. An object or a text or an idea can be cleaved apart, so that parts of it can be used differently from the whole. A person can erupt verbally, even physically, to communicate what would otherwise remain unsaid. Violence doesn't necessarily have an object, but harm always does. As a director, then, I must be willing to embrace violence as a quality of creativity, but I do not have to accept harm as a consequence.

I think about the Buddhist principle of non-harming, which I learned about on a silent meditation retreat: to harm another being, whether it is a child or a chihuahua or a cockroach, is to ignore our common aspiration for happiness. It violates the essential truth of our interdependence. Some violations are so flagrant that harm is immediately evident, but others are trickier. Harm is not always easy to identify. It is often imperceptible, invisible to the eye and ear and hand, sometimes undetectable at first even to its victim. It may hide for awhile, like some kind of moral parasite, waiting until well after exposure to show its symptoms.

So, as I make theater, how do I gauge what is a necessary violence, and what, in fact, is harm?

As a regular part of my job, I ask performers to act and reenact scenes of trauma, as victims and perpetrators. I ask designers and dramaturgs to read and view research about the most horrifying extremes of human behavior. I ask assistants and interns—often very young people, high school or college age—to organize and interpret this research. I ask artists to create objects, clothing, and scenic environments that bring these traumatic events into physical life.

And even when the subject matter is less extreme, the creative act is violent. As Anne Bogart reminds us, decisions are violent, each one, in the moment of the choice, obliterating all other possible options. The making of a thing transforms the material it is made of. A gesture violates stillness. A song destroys silence. It does not matter how beautifully the gesture moves or how gently the song is sung. Violence is a quality of creativity; in fact, pretending creativity is not violent can be harmful. How do I gauge what in the process of making a play is violence necessary to the work of creation, and what might actually be harming my collaborators or my audiences?

In ancient Rome, the Emperor had a taster—called a Praegustator—responsible for tasting food before it was served to ensure it was safe. I think part of good directing is to take up this Praegustator role; it makes sense not to ask anyone else to consume what I haven't tried myself. Sometimes this is a matter of practical safety—I've climbed into high places and tight corners, hoisted pulleys and carried heavy objects, to make sure these felt safe for actors and crew—and sometimes it's a more psychological sharing. I'll taste things in my mind: how would I feel wearing that costume in front of 300 people? How many times in a row could I rehearse this scene, before it became too painful to hear that word yelled at me one more time? I am not trying to predict my collaborators' responses, but to fully feel my own. I've found that my palate is more nervous than most, so if I calibrate to my own tolerance, the meal is likely to be safe for all.

Taking up Praegustator role is a public demonstration of my awake-ness to the possibility of harm, and this in itself is beneficial. Making a point of looking for potentially harmful things shows that I care about the effect of the work on my collaborators. By acknowledging that harm can emerge in any process, that no one needs to be blamed or punished for it, but that it must be identified, addressed, and remedied, I foster a sense that concern for well-being can be a collective endeavor. This may lend some reassurance to those individuals who have felt habitually disregarded, who have been made to feel that their harm is incidental to the process of theater-making; it may support them to engage in the process honestly and not defensively, giving them the space to tolerate a wider range of experience and thus, I think, reducing the scope of what might potentially feel—and be—harmful.

When I was working on the world premiere of *Nat Turner in Jerusalem* at New York Theatre Workshop, Nathan Alan Davis' beautiful script called for the actor playing Turner to have his hands and feet shackled through most of play, which took place in a Virginia jail cell the night before Turner's execution. The research on what these shackles should look like, and the decision of which shackles to purchase, the act of exchanging money for these objects, was incredibly disturbing. I remember getting nauseous looking at the links the designer sent me to choose from. When I spoke to my response, the designer, relieved, revealed that she too had been having trouble viewing the images. We had an emotional conversation about our responses to the different objects, allowing that this decision—ostensibly a technical one—had a weight far beyond the aesthetic.

The shackles we ended up purchasing were real objects, not replicas; they arrived in a package from eBay. I don't know where they'd been or what they'd seen, but holding them in my hands, I could feel their dark history. I remember bringing them into our sunny rehearsal room before the actors arrived. I asked the props designer to put the shackles on my hands and feet. I stood in the rehearsal room wearing them. They were cold and heavy. I took a few steps. It was exhausting, humiliating. Tears filled my eyes. I described how it felt to wear the shackles. The designer described how it felt to put them on me. Also present was my assistant, the stage management team, and the fight choreographer. I reminded them that the only Black actor in the room would be wearing these for hours of rehearsal, and that they would need to be fastened onto his hands and feet by non-Black production assistants. We discussed a protocol for using the shackles in rehearsal. The production assistant would offer the actor a chair so that he could be seated if he wished, verbally ask if he was ready, and then kneel respectfully to shackle or unshackle the actor. No other work would be done in the room while the actor was being shackled or unshackled, nor could anyone begin their break. This created a kind of sacred, focused hush in the room during the minute or so it took to perform the task.

The actor, Phillip James Brannon, gave an incendiary performance in that production. He told me once that he liked putting the shackles on because it was truthful, and he likes the truth. I am certain it took a toll for Phillip to rehearse and perform this role, but I think we managed to avoid a massive dose of unnecessary harm to him by sharing the weight and the truth of those shackles across the company. What's more, our process allowed the designers and the stage management team, who are often asked to perform a kind of technically proficient emotional disinterest, to be present with their own truthful response to the material, avoiding the harm that could have accrued to those artists in the absence of such permission.

The Praegustator system isn't perfect. There is, of course, the problem of the Praegustator's own safety. Knowing my own limits in this role, caring for myself so that I might care for others, is consistently the most difficult part. And there are always moments of failure. Emperor Claudius was killed by poison in AD 54 even though all his food was tasted by a eunuch named Halotus—who was suspected in Claudius' murder but somehow managed to keep his job for two more emperors. My failures as Praegustator fortunately haven't been as spectacular as his. I think most have stemmed from failure to pay sufficient attention to my own response to something. The system doesn't work if you feel a slight twinge in your stomach and you ignore it. Then you're at risk of poisoning a whole room full of people.

As the daughter of an Armenian mother and a Jewish father, I grew up expecting that stories related to my cultural heritage would be violent. I became habituated to tales of terrorism and genocide—the ransacking of homes, the brutal rapes and murders, the systematic destruction of ancestral communities—told and retold at a fever pitch, full of horror and grief, indignation and fury. Most of these tellings had what educator and theater-maker Julie Salvorsen calls "an aesthetic of injury," where we are asked to gaze on "deliberately tragic" characters and situations with intense sympathy ("Oh my god, isn't that terrible? That is so sad."). As awful as the stories were, the aesthetic of injury provided a kind of pleasure—a reliable feeling of teary tragedy, like settling into a familiar armchair.

Bertolt Brecht wrote about this kind of pleasure as "culinary"—the

THERE MUST BE HAPPY ENDINGS

pleasure we derive from art that we consume rather than consider, ingest rather than analyze. In Brecht's view, this style of theater exploits the spectators' most easily accessed emotions. If actors "go into a trance and take the audience with them," both artists and audiences are filled up with generalized but powerful emotion—"like some erotic process" where "the element of terror necessary to all recognition is lacking."

In contrast, the most powerful depiction of the Armenian genocide I've seen was an excerpt of a reading of a new play. From what I remember, the Armenian protagonist was living in Beirut in the 1970's, when the terror of Lebanon's civil war brought back a flood of old memories and untold stories of the genocide her family had fled Turkey to escape 60 years earlier. There was violence, trauma and unimaginable suffering in both the past and the present of the play. Though the details of the plot are now fuzzy in my mind, I can feel the impact of the performance as if it were yesterday. The reading was presented simply, with the cast seated at music stands. The cast was made up of all women, clearly of diverse ethnicities, none of whom were Armenian or even Middle Eastern. Some of the actresses had accents, which they did not attempt to disguise. They spoke simply, without hesitation and without tears, making eye contact with the audience, describing these terrible events with an honesty and directness that was disarming and devastating.

Though I no longer remember the name of the play or the writer, I will never forget this performance. Through the voices of Asian, African and Latina women, accented with their native languages, using an unadorned, emotionally restrained performance style, I was able to hear old stories as if they were brand new. In my previous encounters with stories like this, the telling had been so soaked in grief and anger and guilt and pain, that it was hard for me to find my own feelings. In this telling, the violence of the historical events was spacious enough that I could locate my reaction and, indeed, myself. This version of the story began to liberate me from the harm of the "culinary" tellings—which, by separating me from a more complete, more honest response, had actually interrupted my ability to feel myself in relationship to, and thus to metabolize and reckon with, historical and ancestral trauma.

This was a powerful lesson for me as a maker: the revelation that a less emotionally restrained telling of traumatic events could actually be less emotionally evocative and therefore *more* harmful to an audience than a more restrained one. As a maker, it was also clear to me that the latter was more challenging to create. It's much easier to allow performers the pleasure of indulging in the emotions they have worked to recognize and to feel through their characters than it is to pull back each moment to a place of mindful calibration. Brecht writes that the most powerful performance is one which allows the audience to recognize the themes and characters, while at the same time making them seem unfamiliar. To do this, he instructs, performers should not focus on feeling and transmitting the emotional content of the material (after all, "has one the right to offer others a dish one has already eaten?"), but should strive to be completely physically present onstage in their body while speaking. The actor "must not only sing but show a man singing."

When I worked with playwright Lydia Diamond on her play *Harriet Jacobs* at Central Square Theater in Cambridge, one of the first things she said to me was that the text should be performed with "no rage and no pity." Diamond's play, like Jacobs' autobiography on which it was based, included many direct address monologues where characters described their lives as enslaved persons in North Carolina to the audience. Although the details the characters were sharing were grim, and sometimes graphic, Lydia's "no rage no pity" mandate reminded me that there was a difference between what the characters were immediately feeling and expressing, and a larger, external judgment about their circumstances. "No rage no pity" did not mean that these characters did not ever have feelings of anger or sadness. It meant that as artists our perspective on the characters could not be one of "feeling angry *for*" or "feeling sorry *for*."

To speak and to hear traumatic testimony over and over is painful. It is tempting to turn off, to not feel. But it is equally tempting to give into the feeling, to be taken over by it. To be present to the full spectrum of responses that arise in us and to still make sure the text is fully heard, to be direct without being detached—this is the challenge for both actor and director. In most cases, in *Harriet Jacobs*, the monologues were simple reportage. They needed to be delivered clearly and unsentimentally. This isn't to say that the characters or the actors couldn't feel and show emotion, only that the performances needed to leave the audience room to discover their own response to the content.

Lydia told me about a time that she had gone to see a play about slavery at a regional theater, a beautiful production of a nuanced script, with very talented actors, but where "no rage, no pity" was not the prevailing tone of the performances. There were skilled, virtuosic performances, but in the service of a familiar, sentimental version of Black life. The audience leapt to their feet afterwards. "All those white people standing up like, 'oh my god, slavery was so bad! It really was so terribly bad!' and clapping and crying," Lydia observed. "Those actors thought they got a standing ovation, but it was really a *standing slavation*."

In this kind of performance, either the performer is feeling so much that there is little room left for the audience to feel, or the performance is aimed so intently at one particular response that we end up in tears—and on our feet, clapping—without fully understanding why. The most significant risk, and the one that makes this kind of performance potentially harmful, is that in a performance fueled by rage and pity, emotionality encourages the audience to disconnect, to see the trauma onstage as happening *to* a distant other, rather than as *produced by* a damaging system in which we all participate. Jung wrote that sentimentality is the superstructure erected on brutality—the pretty facade that hides the ugly thing from view. A sentimental

THERE MUST BE HAPPY ENDINGS

performance conceals the brutality of the system.

In addition to the risk to the audience, there's also a risk to the performer—especially performers who, like the actors in *Harriet Jacobs*, share an aspect of traumatic history with the characters they portray. An artist can come to believe and repeat the insufficient representation. Gayle Pemberton writes about the particular risk that African American performing artists face in relationship to DuBois' double-consciousness. In an essay called "O Porgy! O Bess!" Pemberton wrestles with her own conflicted love for the classic "folk opera" written by two Jewish men, struggling with how Black artists might approach the singing of a work that presents a reductive, sentimental portrait of Black experience. Black performers, she writes, "run the risk of sentimentalizing their own lives by internalizing the white response to the sentimental presentation of Black life."

The production of double consciousness is so successful, Pemberton observes, that when asked to portray the truth of their own experience, Black artists may offer up a broad, stereotypical, sentimental rendition, that actually *feels* truthful to them. Black artists attempting to perform a nuanced and truthful portrait of Black life are up against a particular artistic version of double-consciousness, amplified and reaffirmed by actor training, audience responses, and decades of American popular art. The artist must first battle her own internalized double-bind, fighting to access an un-veiled truth within, and then must somehow perform that truth in a way that can transcend the gaze of an American audience, practiced in Du Bois' "amused contempt and self-pity," to reach together for something less familiar.

Pemberton writes that such transcendence is possible only through the act of "good singing"—by which she meant the kind of virtuosic performance given by Leontyne Price on her favorite *Porgy and Bess* recording. The quality of the singing must be excellent for a transcendent performance to occur, but the skill of the singer by no means guarantees it. Perhaps it needs a marriage of Pemberton's "good singing" with Brecht's "not only sing, but show a man singing", avoiding Salverson's "aesthetic of injury" and leaning into Diamond's "no rage, no pity."

Harriet Jacobs was performed by an ensemble of Black actors playing both Black and white characters in Jacobs' life. When an actor transformed from a Black character to a white one, he or she donned a pair of white gloves. In the moment of transformation, the actor stood, holding the glove, grounded in Blackness, looking out at the audience, fully present and aware. They held the glove, looked at it, saw it clearly, and breathed into the gesture, showing us the feeling of their hand entering the glove, and then exhaling into a transformation, a new character, a different body. It was a simple gesture, it did not stop or even really pause the storytelling, but it did show the seams. It was elegant and skillful, beautiful without being sentimental, easy without being obvious. The gesture in itself was a standing-next-to; it made visible not only the transformation from one character to another, but the act of performance itself. It flagged for the audience, "Here a choice has been made. We have thought about the difference between these two characters. About the difference between an actor and a character. We have thought about what it means for this actor to transform into these characters."

This kind of triply-aware performance has the potential not only to avoid harming artists and audiences, but, perhaps to do even more—to provide a healing reckoning. In this kind of performance, we can have a direct encounter with our relationship to traumatic histories, to suffering and the memory of suffering.

Listening to Leontyne Price sing *Porgy and Bess*, Pemberton hears something happen, something apart from the given circumstances of the material and even the performance—"the singers, as representative stereotypes, sang through the stereotypes to transform them, to transcend the art, and even an enthusiastic audience's approval, to reveal a truth through lies that breaks the double bind and announces a self-created Black identity."

⌒

Shortly after we got engaged, my now-wife asked me, "Why do you direct so many plays about the Black experience?"

The first time Candice asked this question, I talked about working at a Black theater, how that had informed my aesthetic and connected me to a group of collaborators. As an American, I said, I felt a responsibility to grapple with the legacy of slavery, with the foundational assumption of white supremacy—which caused my immigrant ancestors to labor to be perceived as white, to both tacitly and explicitly denigrate Blackness, so that they might receive the benefits rather than suffer the injuries of an oppressive system. And I believed in MLK's interrelated structure of reality, that "whatever affects one directly, affects all indirectly," that—in the words of Emma Lazarus, the Jewish immigrant who wrote the famous poem on the Statue of Liberty—"until we all are free, we are none of us free."

The second time she asked, I was defensive. I might have said something like, "I told you already!" I might have repeated my previous answers, the tone of my voice rising slightly.

My answers were true, but they were incomplete. She asked again. My wife is not one to settle for an incomplete answer. "What are you getting out of it?," she asked. "What about Armenian and Jewish stories? Are you sad you haven't gotten to direct plays about your own experience?"

I stopped. Maybe some of the tension dropped from my shoulders. Yes, I said. I was frustrated and sad that I hadn't had the opportunity to direct plays directly connected to my heritage. I've seen maybe three professional productions of Armenian plays. Many of the plays I've encountered about the Jewish experience in America seemed to focus on a kind of New York-y, intellectual Jewishness that didn't reflect my life or my family. And in terms of my mixed ethnic identity—forget about it.

At the same time, it was true that I compulsively returned to African American plays; I found my own emotions most accessible in relationship to those stories. I was able to access rage, grief, pain—once removed. Candice kept repeating and deepening her question because she could see that I was engaged in a kind of appropriative practice. I was practicing being in relationship to histories of trauma, I was leaning on Harriet Jacobs and Lydia Diamond and Nathan Alan Davis to rehearse the possibility of encounter. It is evident in the pages of this book, as my work and my thinking evolves in concert with—aided by—my connection to Black stories, Black artists, Black institutions.

But it was more than that. My *leaning* had the effect of collapsing those individual Black people and their real experiences into a concept of "Blackness" that could stand in for the historical trauma narrative more generally. I could use the "Black experience" as a kind of trauma shorthand for oppression, persecution, dehumanization. This use of a Blackness as symbol of trauma is common in the Unites States, but is not unique. To use one close-to-home example: of the small number of plays by Middle Eastern writers currently being produced at major theaters in the US, many take as their subject the trauma of

Muslim characters, but are written by playwrights who are not themselves Muslim—a similar kind of leaning and collapsing, and perhaps a similar kind of avoidance.

My proximity to someone else's stories of trauma let me stand on the banks of my own traumatic history without plunging in, without abandoning myself to a current that, I feared, might pull me under. "Blackness" seemed to offer a lamp, a bridge, a ship—a way for me to encounter the waters, a structure or a vessel that might be able to take me to a place I longed and feared to go.

I was standing there open handed, with deep compassion, with honest attention, with respect and humility. But because I hadn't fully understood why I was there, what I had come for, I could have caused—might have caused…probably did cause—harm. Nothing—no one—else could light my way or carry me across this water. I had to do it myself.

I read the above passage to Candice. She said, "You aren't standing on the banks of the river. That's an illusion."

I looked at her blankly.

"You sound like a damsel in distress," she said. "Like a blond girl in a white dress, standing so innocently, so tentatively on the banks of the river, trying not to get hurt, trying not to feel any pain, waiting for a strong Black man to come and carry you across, like 'It's alright, missy, I know these here waters. You'll be safe with me.'"

"Yeah," I said. "I think that's kind of what I'm saying."

"But it's an illusion," she said, sitting up and leaning forward, "*being on the bank is an illusion.*"

"Oh," I said. "I'm already in the water?"

"You're already in the water," she said, "and you're not an innocent girl in a white dress. You're covered in blood. You've been beat to shit. And you've had to fight and claw and struggle to survive."

"And now I'm desperate, and I'm clinging to the raft of 'Blackness' because I'm drowning."

"You're clinging to it to avoid your own pain. You feel like you're drowning, not only in the trauma of your own heritage, but in the mystery of it—the distant intellectual knowing, the secrets, the way it hasn't been told. The specific trauma of Black people is on display in a concrete, real way every day in this country and that becomes something you can grab onto."

"So the river is not only my own trauma but the ways I'm cut off from that," I said, my chest tight, my underarms clammy, "and I think the raft is a vehicle to myself."

"Yes," my wife said, and then paused, looking hard at me, "But what you think is a raft is actually a person, floating near you in this trauma river, and in your attempt to save yourself, you're pushing them down."

I picture my battered, drowning body. I picture the tangled history inside it. It holds a people whose Christian identity made them the targets of an ethnic cleansing at the hands of Muslims, *and* a people whose Jewish identity made them the targets of an ethnic cleansing at the hands of Christians, who have now gone on to severely restrict and violate the human rights of Muslims and others, including Christian Armenians, in Israel.

I can feel the legacies of genocide, the harm of denial and erasure. I become aware that these things are, in this moment, painful to me. And they still feel mysterious, slightly out of reach. And that is painful too. I understand that these feelings will never be simple or clear, they will never be fully unpacked. Maybe the best I can hope for is to make as much of myself as possible available to be looked at, to be heard. Maybe in that availability, I find myself floating. I look to my right, and to my left. I see that there are so many other people floating in this river with me.

⌒

In my favorite passage of *The Life of the Drama*, Eric Bentley discusses why, and when, we feel we have had a "momentous experience" in the theater. Some of it, he says, has to do with our emotional experience, with what we feel the "import" of the play to be. Then:

> *If part of this conviction derives from what the play means, another part derives from the mere fact that it means. Meaningfulness is in itself momentous for human beings, as they discover, a contrario, whenever life has no meaning for them. All art serves as a lifebelt to rescue us from the ocean of meaninglessness—an extraordinary service to perform.*

I both love and doubt this final sentence. I love the image—a play, like a kind of art-tether, belting us to a sense of meaning, even as we are tossed by the waves of meaninglessness. (It took me years to look up "lifebelt" and find out it was just a British way of saying "life preserver.") And I doubt whether it can be true. Is it possible that *all* art—really, all of it?—can perform this crucial rescue? What if it is bad art? What if it is harmful art? I keep returning to this question in my mind. I don't know the answer. I do know that, over and over again, I have turned to a play to help me make sense of the world.

When we make a play—actor, director, designer, stage manager—we find ourselves in its suffering and in its joy. It's one of the most compelling reasons to continue to make theater— the constant empathetic exercise. Over and over, we take up somebody else's story and we find ourselves in it.

This is inevitable, and it is beautiful. And it can also, sometimes, be harmful. Sometimes the very power of our empathetic relating risks doing harm to the story's subject—Hudes' Puerto Rican characters, Harriet Jacobs, Armenians in Beirut—by collapsing it, overpowering it, fetishizing it. Sometimes, too, we risk doing harm to ourselves, because this empathetic response may be an elision of our own history. In the middle of the process, how do we determine when we are in the midst of an intolerable harm, and when the work is a necessary violence? I'm not sure there is any way to know with certainty, but I do know this is the kind of virtuosity I strive for, and that it is my work to hold the space so that my collaborators can strive for it, too—the good singing that makes us all more present.

Candice and I got married in Provincetown, in a ceremony that began with us jumping the broom—a ritual calling back to vows made in the slave quarters, and a reminder that not so long ago our inter-racial, same gender union would not have been legally sanctioned. Then my cousin sang the Hayr Mer—the Lord's Prayer in Armenian. At the end of the ceremony, Candice's friend Drey stepped forward with a glass wrapped in a napkin. "It is a Jewish custom to end the wedding ceremony with the breaking of a glass," he said. "Some say that the breaking of the glass symbolizes the irrevocable change in the lives of the couple standing before us; others say it reminds us that life is so fragile that the couple should enjoy every day as if it were their last together. The breaking of the glass also serves as a reminder of the destruction and oppression that has been experienced by your Jewish, African, African-American and Armenian ancestors and that is still being experienced today by many people in this country and around the world. Even in a moment of such great joy, we are asked to remember that there is still pain and suffering in the world and that we have a responsibility to turn towards it, acknowledge it and do our best to be present with it."

We held hands and crushed the glass under our heels; everyone yelled "Mazel tov!" and we danced out to Stevie Wonder.

The next day, as we watched the September sun set over Cape Cod Bay as a married couple, Candice recalled the words her father had spoken in our ceremony. He said that he was thinking about his grandmother, Big Mama, who was born just after the end of slavery. He thought she'd be happy on our wedding day. "You two are the future of love," he'd said. Candice told me that she thought some of the work we were doing together—the hard work of coming to understand each other and ourselves, the reckoning with the legacy of slavery and white supremacy and class disparity and immigration and genocide and the construction of gender and the failure of intersectional feminism and whatever else—the weaving and unraveling of all of that between two human beings—was bigger than us.

"We are doing this work on behalf of the collective," she said. "We are carrying a part of the labor of this country, the hard work that needs to be done, here, between us."

—

Sometimes it happens this way too: the play is about falling in love, and the actors are themselves falling in love. The play is about becoming an adult, stepping into a new space of responsibility, and it teaches the actor how to do that. The play is about coming out to your parents, and one of the actors comes out to their mother when she comes to see the show. The mother loves the show, and she loves her kid. The play has changed something forever in their lives.

Making theater changes *me*. By fighting to hold a space of truth and honesty, it makes me more myself. Through striving to hold a compassionate container, it asks me to be more present in the world, to share more of myself than I otherwise might. It makes me more alive in the world and more alive *to* the world. It is the way I craft living meaning in this disintegrating universe.

The vessel, the free passage, the light.

The Empty Circle

I am four or five years old. I am dreaming, and in the dream, there is the most perfect candy cane in front of me, its red and white helix shining with vivid, mouthwatering beauty. I reach out to take the candy. As I do, I am aware for the first time of the boundary between sleep and wakefulness. I have the sense of myself in the bed, in my room; I remember and understand that I am waking up from my afternoon nap. As my fingers close around the candy cane, I can actually feel the object in my hand—the polished surface, the gentle weight of it. I realize that I have the power to transport the candy cane out of my dream and into my bedroom. I know that I must wake up very slowly, very deliberately, taking it with me, allowing it to gently materialize under my waking hand. I am slowly, slowly, slowly, willing this object to make the journey with me when my father opens my bedroom door. Bright hallway light spills in, he calls my name, and the candy cane dissolves in my outstretched fist. I am awake, holding nothing. I believed then, and will likely always believe, that if I had not been interrupted—five more seconds, ten more seconds!—I would have sat up in bed, awake and awestruck, holding in my hand something from another world.

In his essay on "Quickness" from *Six Memos for the Next Millennium*, Italo Calvino relates the story of an aging

Charlemagne, who fell under an enchantment that caused him to passionately love a young girl, even after her death. The cause of the enchantment was a ring, hidden under her tongue. The ring was discovered and removed by the Archbishop; as soon as it was in his hands, Charlemagne instantly fell madly in love with him. The Archbishop then hurriedly threw the ring into a lake. Charlemagne refused to leave its shores, "his eyes fixed on Lake Constance, in love with the hidden abyss." Calvino offers that the passage of the ring links an otherwise random series of people and events, girl to Archbishop to lake, exerting "a kind of force field that is in fact the territory of the story itself." The narrative is fueled by "the drive of desire toward a thing that does not exist, a lack or absence symbolized by the empty circle of the ring."

My childhood dream has not waned in its ability to awaken in me vivid feelings of anticipation and loss. Was it my first and best chance to make something invisible visible? Having failed in that primal moment, how can I know whether my desire was driving towards a *real object*—something so precious that it takes form only at the threshold—or, like Charlemagne's, towards a lack or absence? Is it the ring I seek, or the empty space inside the circle?

As a young person I always nursed a preoccupation with existential desire. I fell in love with a fierce and immediate frequency. My loves were characterized by delirious joy at first encounter and bitter tears upon separation, followed by wistful enshrinement of the beloved in sacred memory and the longing—ever unfulfilled—for reunion. The objects of my affection included, among others, a puppy on the street in Rome, a Joseph Cornell box in the Seattle Art Museum, a girl on my high school lacrosse team who sang Joni Mitchell, and a lake in the Cascades I visited once with my family. Like Charlemagne, I sat by its shore bewitched, composing poems to the unparalleled beauty of its curving banks, the light on the water. Recently I asked my mother about the childhood trip to this lake. She was perplexed. She remembers the lake as an average place in an average recreation area, a body of water created in the 1950's to power a hydroelectric dam.

In these stories, I sound a lot like Charlemagne, chasing the empty space inside the ring, seeing the object in front of me only as a vessel for my own enchantment, fueled by the drive of desire towards a thing that does not exist. What was I following, from puppy to artwork to teenage girl to lake? Each time, I felt myself at a threshold, as in my dream, with the possibility of grasping a revelation from another world. Each time, I was left alone with my own longing.

Am I like Charlemagne?

Making theater, too, began as an exercise in enchantment for me. My father is a playwright and a director; I used to accompany him to rehearsals. The spaces where he made theater—rehearsal rooms with tall, drafty windows; black box studios with chipped paint and folding chairs; auditoriums with blue velvet seats—were full of magic. As long as I can remember, entering spaces like these has made my heart swell against my chest, my breath drop down into my knees. And I've always been curious about how my concrete, practical father—the dream-waker who made the candy cane disappear—could move through such shimmering realms, seemingly unaffected. He sees making a play as a series of problems to be solved. I see it as an attempt to make an image in the mind's eye into a real object or experience, just as in my dream—an attempt to bring something over the threshold from invisible to visible.

My father is definitely not like Charlemagne.

And to his point, in theater, the empty space is not an abstraction. It is very real—cold and echoing, strewn with bent nails and half-used rolls of black gaff tape—just waiting to be filled by a performance. *The Empty Space* is so real that it is the title of one of the most seminal and beautiful books on theater-making, a book my father gave to me when I was in college. Any empty space, Peter Brook writes, can be a stage, any action there makes it into a theater.

My father and I both chose to try to make a living in this empty space, even if for different reasons. For me, making a career out of making theater is a peculiar cocktail of imagination and vocation. I am hired based on my ability to achieve sublime truth in a make-believe world, to contain and express what is most private and meaningful in a room full of strangers, to replicate and reify the most internal, intimate human processes, night after night. Maybe it's more accurate to say that I am hired based on how successfully I can convince someone else of my ability to do those things—since there is no physical evidence of this ability, no lasting artifact. I cannot point to something that's mine, I can't pick it up and hold it in my hand. I don't compose the music or build the costumes; I don't write a script, or construct a character—other people make those things, playwrights and actors. My artistry is not invention but stewardship. My work is, mostly, invisible and ephemeral.

I convene a group of creative minds. There's a conversation; I hold space for it. I attend to the collaborative process—in a way that's in line with my values, with compassion and rigor. I build a container that provides the space for others to do their best work. The result of this process is the crystallization of some meaning that my watchfulness has nurtured and affirmed—hopefully a meaning that coheres and resonates for the viewer, lifting up out of the noise of our lives into a moment of grace, of order, one of Calvino's "privileged points in which we seem to discern a design or perspective."

In the beginning of the process, my directing work feels fueled by that familiar "drive of desire": I long to know, to understand, to be connected, to be part of something. But sometimes, as I negotiate the minutiae of auditions, design budgets and schedules, I fear that my desire for the *result* of theater-making—the meaning, the understanding, the connection, the "something" that is generated—is greater than my desire for the *process* of theater-making. Even the rehearsal room—that sacred, intoxicating space of discovery—sometimes becomes a laborious and heavy place. I feel nervous (all these people want me to tell them what to do?) and exhausted (*really* watching and *truly* listening takes so much energy!) and sometimes bored (oh no! Am I bored because the play is boring and I'm a bad director?) which leads me to pure terror. *The play will be bad, no meaning will be made, it will all be for naught, the reviews will be terrible and no one will ever hire me again.* I often feel longing for other things while I'm in rehearsal—a hot bath, a long walk, a good meal, a quiet nap, or a less-complicated story. Oh how I *wish* I were snuggled up on the couch, watching *Top Chef* and eating tacos, instead of here at this boring, exhausting, terrifying rehearsal!

It's at this point that I start to suspect that perhaps I am, in fact, nothing like Charlemagne—not in a practical and clarifying way, like my father, but in a less admirable, more shameful way. Perhaps I am standing by the shores of the lake not to puzzle out the solution to a problem, and not out of love or enchantment, but merely because I've stood there before. I'm trying to manufacture a feeling I think I remember, but without purpose or meaning, fueled only by anxiety, an urgency to return to a previous state. I become increasingly frightened and distressed. At any moment I could be unmasked as an impostor and a fraud; someone is sure to barge into the room and interrupt, leaving me disoriented, awake, and holding nothing. I should quit, I think, and get a real job. This is the last show. This is the last time I will stand on these shores feeling this feeling but wishing I were feeling that other feeling that maybe wasn't ever even a real feeling.

Eventually, sets and lights and costumes appear; the empty space is filling. I come early and stay late to stare at the half-assembled set, dizzy from the smell of fresh paint. As audiences start to trickle in—dress rehearsal, previews—I get a flutter in my chest, a weight in the pit of my stomach. The enchantment creeps back in. Relief. Sometimes I can see the performance as if I am floating above it, aware of its internal logic, the skeletal web of meaning that it weaves, night after night—or that it *wants* to weave, that it *could* weave, if the weaving were good enough. My job, those precious days between technical rehearsals and opening night, is to nurture that web, to gild its delicate strands with silver and gold, to make them visible, to make them strong.

Watching each run of the show during that time, I *long*, a painful, achy, hold-my-breath kind of longing, for clarity, for synthesis. I long for the story to be told, for the rise and fall of each moment to feel inevitable, for each image to resonate with unexpected but undeniable truth. When images disintegrate, when moments stumble, I long to repair them. I must repair them.

I write pages of notes. I call actors on the phone. I have emergency brainstorming lunches with designers. I text the playwright.

I do some more research. I rehearse. I rehearse. I rehearse. I strain to achieve Calvino's "inner inevitability" which "mark[s] every image as form and as meaning, as a claim on the attention and a source of possible meanings." I want it to be beautiful. I startle awake at 4 a.m. with a new, great idea that turns out not to be a great idea… but as long as I'm up, I bake cookies for the costume shop.

Opening night, exhausted by desire, I sit in the audience. I try to simply be in the room with other people, watching. The final cue is called. Applause. A party. And then, it's over. My job is done.

Quite often, in the queer vacancy that follows, I ask myself whether I will continue to choose this, whether I could—or would—do something else. The empty space ahead begs the question of what will come to fill it. It could be filled with gardening or babies, teaching or writing. Why make theater? The truth is that there is no reason, really. Theater-making is incidental; it is a site of discovery, not the object of the longing. Theater-making is what I've chosen; it is a circumstance that brings me to the shores of the lake, but it is not the feeling that makes me stay.

In fact, sometimes I feel myself very close to making another choice—biting into a just-picked strawberry, seeing a student's eyes light up, or holding my friend's newborn son—as in the dream of the candy cane, I can feel my fingers closing around something uncloseable. I am touching the surface of a thing with no surface. It is there in the garden, in the classroom, in the warm brow of the sleeping infant, in the cab to the airport before sunrise, on the runway. In that privileged threshold between the dream of the night and the night itself lives a feeling that is true in both worlds—a rush of inner inevitability, threatening to arouse, and thus expose, the truth of the ring, the myth of the empty circle.

I can feel it everywhere.

And yet I keep returning to the theater.

I imagine Lake Constance—it looks just like a lake in the Cascades at dusk. I am sitting on a rock outcropping on the eastern side. Across from me, standing on the other shore, is Charlemagne. He is backlit by the fading sky so I can't make out his features; I only know it is him because I can see his crown glinting in the pink of the sunset. We face each other across the empty circle. Though, of course, it is not empty. It is full of lake, and of the enchantment that has brought us both there.

At the bottom of the circle of the lake, the circle of the ring; in both, the space of endless possibility, the labor of the threshold married to the enchantment of the threshold, the frame that might tell us where to look, how to see, through which we might glimpse a flash of shocking beauty—something so rare and so powerful that, in our waking lives, we are compelled to search for it, to seek to re-encounter it.

I'm suddenly aware of the possibility that it is not Charlemagne on the other side of the lake but my father. I'm not sure why he is wearing a crown, but maybe there are a lot of things he does that I don't understand. And he has been known to dress strangely.

He couldn't have known what he would destroy by turning on the light, by calling me out of my dream. "Megan, time to wake up!"

It might be time to forgive him for this loss. After all, in the moment he snatched something away from me, he gifted me something too. In jarring me awake, he instilled in me the original longing, the drive of desire towards something that may or may not exist, an endless source of delight and heart-ache and mystery that has become my life's work. In his calm, practical insistence on waking, was my father in fact the unwitting sorcerer who placed me under enchantment? Perhaps his pragmatism opened up the space for my dream. Does it, in the end, really matter? However we came to it, however differently we inhabit it, we arrived at a shared space. And we continue to arrive, each time we gather—parent, child, artist, audience—to fill a room with our shared longing.

The empty space cannot be held in your hand. But at its best, perhaps, it can give to a room full of people the gift of the threshold—the sensation of another, possible world, so close we can feel it. Standing together at the portal, dreaming of possibility, the collective dream that tells us something about ourselves that can only be known in a space of enchantment. The desire born there might fade away when the lights come on—or, if we allow it, it might follow us into waking life, the fuel we need to continue to hold the channel open. In seeking a return to the beauty of the dream, we find beauty all around us, we work to protect it, to replicate it, to share it—and then one day, if we're lucky, we realize we have spent our lives bringing more beautiful things into the world.

Contact

Contradictions are our hope!
− Bertolt Brecht

*If hope isn't forced to encounter the worst
possibility, then it's a lie.*
− Tony Kushner

It's a short drive from my home to where Harriet Jacobs and her daughter Louisa Matilda rest side by side on Clethra Path in Mt. Auburn Cemetery in Watertown, MA. I can find the plot easily from the front entrance, have made the trip many times, in many seasons, to offer a prayer and puzzle over the inscriptions. Harriet's gravestone reads, "Patient in tribulation, fervent in spirit serving the Lord." Louisa selected the epitaph, adapted from Paul's Epistle to the Romans. The original Bible verse has a list of instructions, including: "Abhor that which is evil; cleave to that which is good… fervent in spirit; serving the Lord; Rejoicing in hope; patient in tribulation."

Crouching there on the damp ground in front of their headstones, I've wondered: what does Louisa's reversal of the lines, and her omission of the connecting sentiment, "rejoicing in hope," mean? As she laid her mother to rest, did Louisa reject "rejoicing"? Did "hope" ring false? In her biography of

Harriet Jacobs, Jean Fagan Yellin hypothesizes that the rephrasing speaks to a sense of despair Louisa may have felt at the condition of African Americans at the end of the 19th century. At the time of Jacobs' death in 1897, reconstruction was already a distant memory. The year before, Plessy vs. Ferguson had ratified segregation and Jim Crow by declaring that separate could be equal.

I feel an ancestral connection to Harriet and Louisa Jacobs that is difficult to explain. Surely it is not only because I once did a play based on Harriet Jacobs' autobiography, *Incidents in the Life of a Slave Girl.* I have done many plays, about many people. Whatever the reason, I keep coming back here to Watertown, to Lot 4389 on Clethra Path.

Watertown also happens to be where my Armenian great-grandparents settled when they arrived in this country, the place my grandmother was born. At the end of her life my grandmother lived in the Washington DC area, but she wanted to be buried back in Watertown. Harriet, too, lived in the nation's capital at the end of her life, and was returned to Watertown after her death. This small parallel pleases me.

My grandmother was born in 1912—fifteen years after Harriet's death, five years before Louisa's, and 42 years before *Brown vs. The Board of Education* would deal the first substantial blow to *Plessy vs. Ferguson.* She did not write an autobiography, but she did write—countless greeting cards, brief letters on thin paper, brightly colored postcards. I have a plastic bag full of her writing from grade school, which I rescued from the recycling pile at my aunt's house. The penmanship is beautiful and the voice is bright, clear and diligent. None of it reveals the other ways I suspect my grandmother was like Harriet—that sometimes a dark cloud lingered over her and was difficult to shake. I wish she had written about that, but she didn't—as far as I know.

My grandmother died about a month after I graduated from college. I remember her disappointment that she was not well enough to make the trip to see it in person, and how proud she was nonetheless. I used to write her postcards, knowing that she would rather get a short note from me frequently than a long one once in awhile. For years after she died, I would buy postcards wherever I went, stacking them up in my desk drawer. She must have done something similar—also in that desk drawer is her greeting card collection, which someone passed on to me. She had cards for all of us, for every occasion. She was prepared for years of birthdays and anniversaries and Valentines Days. I can imagine what she might have written, the dollar bills she would have slipped in the envelope. I'm less sure what she would have made of my life, now—my marriage, my career, my politics, my trips to visit the graves of two Black women I never knew.

———

What was Louisa thinking when she memorialized her mother as she did?

"Patient in tribulation, fervent in spirit serving the Lord."

Does the re-write of St. Paul speak to, as Yellin says, a sense of despair? And if so, was the despair Louisa's or her mother's? Was she writing for her audience—us? Or was she writing for herself? Was she compelled by financial constraint to limit her words? Did she intentionally leave a mystery for us to puzzle over? Or, perhaps, did she simply misremember the passage?

I imagine taking up what Louisa left out: *Rejoicing in hope.* What if *I* were buried under that? What kind of ending would that be?

"*In this chaotic and unjust world,* she rejoiced in hope.*"

Is that true? And even if it could be true—is it fair, is it even ethical, to allow *hope* the final word?

I want to say yes. I've always wanted to, and at the end of writing these pages, I can feel that impulse in me still. To jump up, to shout it from the rooftops—*yes, yes, we must rejoice.* Like Jill Dolan, we must find pleasure and inspiration in being alive and in the same room together; like Gayle Pemberton, we must believe in the power of good singing to reveal a truth through lies that breaks the double bind. Like Hedwig, we must be glam and punk and broken and whole, singing "Lift up your hands!"

At age ten I used to page through our appealingly thick

Bulfinch's Mythology. It did not include the tale of Hedwig's spherical people divided, but it did have another creation myth I liked. Prometheus, aided by his brother Epimetheus, stole fire from the gods. To punish them, the gods created Pandora, the first woman—the story has some troubling implications already, though I didn't notice at age ten—and gave her as a "gift" to Epimetheus. Pandora promptly opened a forbidden jar in his house, from which escaped "a multitude of plagues for hapless man"—physical illness, ills of the mind, "envy, spite, and revenge." She quickly closed the jar, but it was too late—the evils had all escaped, save one: hope.

The tale is confusing. Even Bulfinch was confused: "how could *hope*, so precious a jewel as it is, have been kept in a jar full of all manner of evils?" Is it possible that to understand the myth, we have to consider that hope is just as bad as everything else in that jar? Are we willing to imagine that the perils of unchecked hope are as great as the perils of any other unchecked evil?

And there are so many unchecked evils.

Harriet Jacobs lived under the brutal system of American chattel slavery. She was held in bondage by a man who terrorized her with sexual advances from the age of twelve, who brutalized her family and friends. His threats forced her to run without her children, to remain hidden under the roof of a shed, in a space no larger than the space under a dining table, for seven long years. And he never stopped pursuing her, long after her escape, even after the end of the war and the end of slavery.

Jacobs called her tiny hiding place her "loophole of retreat."
Even within that space of constraint, she was, she wrote, freer
than she could be anywhere else as long as slavery existed. From
there, she peered through a peephole to see her children playing
in the yard below. Her son once heard her sneeze and, with
the imaginative clarity of a small child, instantly knew that his
mother was not in the North after all, but five feet above his
head. He led his sister Louisa and their playmates away from
the shed so that she would not be discovered. He kept her secret.

The peephole. The sneeze. The extraordinary tension of longing
and contact. My grandmother's unwritten autobiography. The
account I will never read of *her* dark nights or lonely days, her
joys and sorrows. She was three years old at the beginning of
the Armenian genocide. She must have lived her entire life in its
shadow. How did she manage to make sense of the unchecked
evil that spilled across the land of her parents and grandparents and every other known and unknown ancestor—an ocean
away from Watertown on the map, but surely much closer in
her mind? Or maybe not. Maybe it felt distant compared to
the immediacy of her of own losses. Her father died when she
was eight years old—not in a genocide, but in the middle of
Sunday dinner. She used to go to visit his grave every week after
church, and on holidays. The flat granite marker she now shares
with my grandfather is at the foot of her father's headstone—in
the very place, I imagine, that she must have stood time after

time, wishing him a merry Christmas before going home to open her presents.

———

Contact happens across a void, literal or metaphorical, without erasing the void. It is neither the bridge nor the moat, but the place where something briefly, temporarily reaches toward something that reaches back. It is the breathtaking moment in *E. T.*—the first movie I ever saw—when two beings from different worlds touch their index fingers together, generating a tiny point of light. It can be an embrace, or kiss—the transgressing lips of Pyramus and Thisbe, through the wall's crack—but it can also be jarring, it can be violent. It can leave us unsettled, or even unhinged.

Julie Salverson writes of the possibility of a performance operating as "an ethical space in which a relationship between detachment and contact occurs." When certain conditions are met, a performance can be an experience of, or at least a representation of, an authentic encounter. This kind of encounter demands that, as Salverson writes, we emerge from behind the safety of our masks of solidarity in order to "speak to" and not "speak of" an Other. When a performance manages to create the open, unsentimental space where an authentic encounter can take place, the results can be breathtaking.

Years ago, I saw a production of *Annie* at Trinity Repertory

Company in Providence, directed by Amanda Dehnert. In this popular musical, the titular flame-haired orphan sheds her miserable past and is adopted into wealth, fame, and happiness. The poverty, abuse, and loneliness in which Annie and the other orphans are trapped at the beginning of the show is subsumed by a fantasy of privileged inclusion that erases their past experience. *Annie*'s exaggerated representation of fusion is a typical musical theater happy ending: it cannot allow the space for contact, it cannot risk the continuing acknowledgment of the void. Yet Dehnert's *Annie* managed to point to all the unresolved questions in our musical happy endings, while also creating a moment of true, heart-stopping contact.

This *Annie* was set in a poor and desperate city; the "orchestra" was a few hungry-looking street musicians wandering around the set. In a desolate orphanage, a little girl wakes up crying from a nightmare. To reassure the child, her friend Annie sings a song of immense longing ("Maybe"). The tyrannical headmistress Miss Hannigan barrels into the room, forcing the orphans to clean although they are starving and tired ("It's a Hard Knock Life"—sounds familiar, right?). In the midst of this, Annie manages to escape, concealed in a laundry truck. The other orphans are ecstatic—now Annie will be able to find her family! Once Annie exits the truck, she finds herself in the middle of the cold and dangerous city. She has no money, nothing to eat, and no way of beginning the search for her parents. It is the middle of the Great Depression, and everyone on the streets is just as destitute as she is. Exhausted and freezing, she finds shelter in an abandoned theater and falls asleep.

The stage is bare and dark, with one little girl asleep in the middle of it. Finally, a friendly dog walks onstage cautiously, also looking for shelter. Annie wakes up. She sees the dog. She smiles. Suddenly, the rest of the musical unfolds in beautiful color—cuddly dog! Daddy Warbucks! FDR! The New Deal! The sun'll come out tomorrow! The events in the musical reach a ludicrous level of fantasy, as Annie is adopted by a doting millionaire and the nation is promised an easy way out of the Great Depression. Everyone is singing and dancing at the happiest of endings. And then the lights fade and the stage empties again. The shiny mansion retreats and we are back on the dim, forbidding streets of the winter city. It grows quiet, and again we see a little girl sleeping in an abandoned theater, huddled against the cold. It's Annie. She's not at Daddy Warbucks' house after all. In a flash we understand that it was all a dream—the dog, the money, the president, the love. But as Annie wakes up, shivering, a friendly dog walks onstage. They look at each other. End of play.

I sobbed. And I leapt to my feet. It was *so* good. And it was so *real*.

As the dog and the girl regarded each other, there was the tug of possibility, which wouldn't have been possible without the circus of musical delight that preceded it; after enjoying the spectacle, I was now implicated in its demise. How could I

207

have watched that? How could I have believed it? What did I really hope for children who, like Annie, have been denied opportunities? What did I hope for all of us, the constellation of Americans who are not Daddy Warbucks, we who long to believe in the dream of a better future while living in the grit of our circumstances? This moment of true contact contained both the pain and the pleasure of the possible: the knowing of what is, alongside the proposal of what might be. The final image violently destroyed and gently offered out the happy ending in the same moment, the moment of contact between girl and dog.

This is perhaps the most satisfying happy ending I have ever experienced in the theater.

And I was one of very few people that did experience it. Lyricist Martin Charnin came to see the show that same night, and soon after threatened a lawsuit if Dehnert did not change her ending. After only a handful of performances, the final image was gone, and with it the acknowledgment of true need and the possibility for true contact. By removing the last-minute revelation that the elaborate musical confection had been Annie's dream, I have to think the production lost the acute honesty that, to me, made it feel so devastatingly real.

Salverson writes that the possibility of making contact in a performance requires "an insistence on engagement based in availability and the willingness to step forward without certainty"; the goal is relationship, not resolution. We are compelled by some distant possibility, some persistent sense of wondering, to reach out for an alien finger; we don't know what will happen next, we only know that whatever happens, it will happen to us. Contact contains the possibility—even the probability—of failure. We may not recognize each other, we may not understand each other, we may even injure each other. Yet we reach out.

I have read *Incidents in the Life of a Slave Girl* more times over than perhaps any other book I own. Harriet Jacobs, through her life, through her book, reached out to me across the veil of time and space. And I reached back. Was I longing for the voices of my own ancestors when I heard hers? I think I was. I also felt undeniably claimed by her as a descendant. I was shaken to the core by our encounter, by my meeting with this singular woman, her words and her ideas, who taught me so much about negotiating my own internal darkness. I became one point of light in a constellation of contact: Lydia Maria Child, the white woman who wrote the forward to *Incidents*, ensuring its publication, but also causing Jacobs' authorial identity to be buried for decades; Jean Fagan Yellin, the professor at Pace University who found a curious document in the archives and dedicated her entire career to restoring Jacobs' rightful place in literary history; Lydia Diamond, the playwright who brought young Harriet to life for a contemporary audience; Kami Smith, the actress who played Harriet in the production I directed and who visited her grave before I did. And perhaps, too—for they must be there, if I am there—the other fierce and complex women of my lineage: my grandmother, my mother, my someday-daughter.

In writing these words, I long to make contact. In the same moment, I despair of making contact. I can write that I am sitting on the porch in the early morning hush, a blanket wrapped around me to guard me from the chill. And even as I write those words, which are at this moment true, I know that by noon the street will be buzzing with the life of the neighborhood, and it will be too hot to sit where I am sitting now. It is as if the passage of a few hours makes my truth into a lie—for as you read these words, or even as I re-read them later, I will no longer be wrapped in a blanket on the porch. And my ideas, which seemed so crisp and dewy in the quiet morning, may have wilted in the afternoon sun. It seems senseless to write anything down, for I am, even now, changing my mind.

And yet, though you can be certain I am no longer where I was at the time of this writing, you might, if you choose, believe that I was once here, just as I believe that at some future moment you will be where you are now, reading these words, or perhaps choosing not to read them. If I believe in your future moment, and you believe in my past moment, then is it too great a stretch for either of us to believe in a collection of alternative moments? A constellation of nows, spread out across the entire span of human history and beyond, in which we are inevitably and inextricably implicated by our curious inquiry, by our willingness to say, "I can imagine you."

Each act—of writing or reading, of making or viewing, of acting or directing—is an act of reaching out to another point in the void, a point from which someone is reaching out to you. The mutual reaching represents an extraordinary collusion across time and space, a combined act of radical faith.

In the availability of one human experience to another human experience, in the twin desires to know and to be known, I find a new kind of hope—somehow both risk and blessing.

Maybe, then, the happy ending is not what creates hope, or defines hopeful art. It is in each moment of potential encounter along the path, and how available we are willing to be, again and again, to the idea that something might be generated there. It is the cold little girl and the hungry dirty dog locking eyes. It is the journey of the ring from one hand to the next, the cross of the horizontal axis with the vertical, the moment where the dream of the night touches the night itself.

I pick up *"rejoicing in hope"* from the cutting room floor where Louisa Matilda Jacobs left it. It is precious to me not only for itself, and not as an antidote to all the evils at loose in the world, but because Louisa has touched it. It connects me to her. And through her, to her mother, and to my grandmother, and to you, who will read this book, and to the people who may some day puzzle over the epigraph on my gravestone, whatever it may be. This is the gift I long for, the breath together across time and space, the mutual availability, the possibility: the moment of contact.

Areas of Order

The universe disintegrates into a cloud of heat, it falls inevitably into a vortex of entropy, but within this irreversible process there may be areas of order... a work of literature is one of those minimal portions in which the existent crystallizes into a form, acquires a meaning.

– Italo Calvino, *Six Memos for the Next Millennium*

ON DIRECTING & MAKING THEATER

Eric Bentley, *The Life of the Drama*

Anne Bogart, *And Then You Act: Making Art in an Unpredictable World*
All of Anne Bogart's books are wonderful. I was especially impacted by this one.

Bertolt Brecht, *Brecht on Theatre*

Peter Brook, *The Empty Space*

Quiara Alegría Hudes, "The High Tide of Heartbreak" (in the October 2018 edition of *American Theatre*)

Willie Reale, *52 Pick Up: A Practical Guide to Doing Theater With Children*
This book details The 52nd Street Project's youth playwriting workshops, adapted from Daniel Judah Sklar's "Playmaking" method.

Julie Salverson, "Taking Liberties: A Theatre Class of Foolish Witnesses" (pages 246-247 of *Research in Drama Education,* volume 13.2, June 2008)
This article was especially impactful, but I love and recommend all of Julie Salverson's writing on performing traumatic testimony.

Sandra G. Shannon and Dana A. Williams, "A Conversation with August Wilson," in *August Wilson and Black Aesthetics*

August Wilson, *The Ground on Which I Stand*. Address originally delivered June 26, 1996 to the 11th biennial Theatre Communications Group National Conference at Princeton University.

August Wilson: The Ground on Which I Stand, Dir. Sam Pollard, PBS film.

Musical Theater

Scott McMillin, *The Musical As Drama: A Study of The Principles and Conventions Behind Musical Shows from Kern to Sondheim*

Stacy Wolf, *A Problem like Maria: Gender and Sexuality in the American Musical* and *Changed for Good: A Feminist History of the Broadway Musical*

Harriet Jacobs

Lydia Diamond, *Harriet Jacobs: A Play*.

Harriet Jacobs and John S. Jacobs, *Incidents in the Life of a Slave Girl: Written By Herself*
I recommend the 2009 Harvard University Press edition edited by Jean Fagan Yellin, which includes Jacobs' brother's narrative as well as some of Jacobs' correspondence.

Jean Fagan Yellin, *Harriet Jacobs: A Life*

Books That Made Me Want To Write a Book

Italo Calvino, *Six Memos for the Next Millennium*
Alexander Chee, *How to Write an Autobiographical Novel*
Jill Dolan, *Utopia in Performance*
Toni Morrison, *Playing in the Dark*
Gayle Pemberton, *The Hottest Water in Chicago*
Elaine Scarry, *On Beauty and Being Just*

ON DHARMA, BUDDHISM & MEDITATION PRACTICE

Ruth King, *Mindful of Race: Transforming Racism from the Inside Out*
Dharma talks by Ruth King, as well as those by Jonathan Foust,
Kate Johnson, Jack Kornfield and La Sarmiento deeply influenced
and grounded me during the writing of this book. You can find them
all on dharmaseed.org as well as elsewhere online and in person.

Rainer Maria Rilke, Anita Barrows, and Joanna Macy. *Rilke's Book
of Hours: Love Poems to God* (New York: Riverhead Books, 2005).
I first heard the Rilke poem cited in *The Old Dark Cloud Comes
Over Me* on the actual radio during *Speaking of Faith* (now one of
my favorite podcasts, *On Being*), in an episode called "The Soul in
Depression"

Rev. Angel Kyodo Williams, Lama Rod Owens, and Jasmine
Syedullah, *Radical Dharma: Talking Race, Love, and Liberation*

AT THE CROSSROADS

Maya Deren, *Divine Horsemen: The Living Gods of Haiti*

John Dewey, *Art As Experience*

Lewis Hyde, *The Gift*

Adrienne Cecile Rich, *The Dream of a Common Language: Poems,
1974 - 1977* and *What is Found There: Notebooks on Poetry and
Politics*

Jeanette Winterson, *Art and Lies*

Candice, for helping me make the space to do this work—not just the early mornings and the late nights, but the space inside me and around me that I never would have created myself. Thank you for pushing me to be the person that could write this book.

R.N., thank you for bringing me to the theater in the first place, and for being my first and best dramaturg. The gifts you've given me outweigh the candy cane many, many times over.

V.A., thank you for loving this book as much as you love me, and for being the worlds best cheerleading section. You always said I was a writer.

Nehassaiu, my highly adaptable sister, thank you for seeing me, even behind the curtains.

Jackie, because I still hear your voice in my head: "A cat with gloves on will catch no mice."

Kira, for gently reminding me that when one assembles, it's good to have some dark colors in the pile.

Dana, Stacy, Noelle, Pirronne, Rachael, Cynthia, Erika, Nehassaiu, Candice, Mom and Dad - for your generous, curious, super-smart reads of essay drafts, and for being the people I trusted enough to ask. Seeing how completely I have you in my corner was one of the most moving parts of this process.

Nambi E. Kelley, Eli Nixon, Jo Dery, Ju-Pong Lin, and all those who I learned from and with in my time at Goddard College.

Marilyn, Carlos, Jen, Sarah: I'm honored to be in your company.

Amanda, Marisa, Debbie, Julie: for the circle of the sangha, and for freeing me from anxiety about imperfection.

My family: Adele, Corinne, and Si, for being willing to have a hard conversation; Alonzo, for the fellowship on the writing road; Brenda, for loving books even more than I do; Jeanne and Alain for cheering my slow progress; Charlotte and Alice, for being, at all times, totally yourselves, and Eric and Laura for making them that way.

Sean Tuten, for traveling a long part of the road with me. This book would not exist without you.

DCM, for giving me extraordinary joy when I needed it most.

KW, for showing me I could survive the darkness.

EMN, for the big feelings. What felt possible then has shaped every step I've taken since.

ACKNOWLEDGMENTS

The artists and theaters I've gotten to collaborate with, especially:

The casts, crews, and creative teams of *Nat Turner in Jerusalem* at New York Theatre Workshop, *Harriet Jacobs* at Central Square Theater and *Hedwig and the Angry Inch* at Perishable Theater/Trinity Rep.

Gus, Carol, and all the kids and adults from my years at The 52nd Street Project.

Maurice, Jonathan, Danny, Veronika and all the performer-writer-thinker-collaborators who have so deeply influenced my thinking. Getting to make stuff with you has made me into me.

Lydia Diamond, Nathan Alan Davis, Eleanor Burgess, Madhuri Shekar, and so many other playwrights who've given me the gift of stepping inside your work and your process. You've taught me more than I can say about writing, collaboration, and faith.

Beth Blickers, for always having all the answers to all my questions.

Debra Wise, Eric Ting, Sean Daniels and the many other institutional leaders who have given me the time and space and support to make theater, and who work so hard with so much heart every single day on behalf of artists and audiences.

My thinking has been profoundly shaped by Buddhist philosophy and by the insight meditation community, and by psychoanalytic theory as introduced to me by my wife, Dr. Candice Crawford-Zakian. In particular, her sharing of the work of Melanie Klein influenced and helped give shape to my thinking about "the split."

Jill Dolan, for *Utopia in Performance*, to which this book, and my theater-making, owes a huge debt.

I am indebted to Margarete Steffin, Ruth Berlau, & Bertolt Brecht, Harriet Jacobs & Jean Fagan Yellin, Jasmine Syedullah, Peter Brook, Italo Calvino, Gayle Pemberton, Julie Salverson, Elaine Scarry, Lisa Kron, Lowry Marshall, Julie VanNoppen, Katy, Wendy, and all of my other teachers along the way.

To Mr. Ito, to Santana, to Marsha, to August, to Black Rep, to Johnny Lee, to Michaelle, to all the artists and institutions gone sooner than we planned: you are with me, always.

And finally, Anne: you've completely changed my life now not once but twice. All the green glitter in this beautiful disintegrating universe is insufficient.

The 3rd Thing 2020 Cohort

Juan Alonso-Rodríguez | 2020 Cover Artist
Ink and graphite drawings from Cuban-born artist Juan Alonso-Rodríguez's *Palm Desert* series reflect the influence on his work of "the organized balance, pattern and symmetry found in nature."

Melissa Bennett | 2020 Land Acknowledgment Writer
The poems that appear at the front of each 2020 title are offered by Indigenous poet Melissa Bennett "as medicine across generations."

Jennifer Calkins | *Fugitive Assemblage*
California, 1983. A woman pulls an IV out of her arm, walks out of the hospital, and starts driving north. *Fugitive Assemblage* is lyric noir rendered through ghostly images and voices conjured out of the trauma of family, of place, of love.

Marilyn Freeman | *The Illuminated Space: A Personal Theory & Contemplative Practice of Media Art*
Expansive and personal, lyrical and analytical, fragmented and fluent, *The Illuminated Space* divines the dialectical nature of time-based art.

Megan Sandberg-Zakian | *There Must Be Happy Endings: On a Theater of Optimism & Honesty*
An artistic coming-of-age story in ten essays, *There Must Be Happy Endings* navigates the ethics of making hopeful art in an unjust and chaotic world.

Carlos Sirah | *The High Alive: An Epic Hoodoo Diptych*
Together *The Light Body* and *The Utterances* transform book into performance space for a mythopoesis of blackness and queerness, of return and foray in this tête-bêche diptych of grief and possibility.

The 3rd Thing is an independent press dedicated to publishing necessary alternatives. Each year we produce a suite of projects that represents our interdisciplinary, intersectional priorities in terms of form, content and perspective. We think of these projects as a cohort in conversation with one another and readers, contributing to our endeavor to create not just beautiful books, but culture.

"The third thing" is the idea that emerges when we use imagination instead of compromise to solve a problem, meet a need, resolve a conflict, answer a question, question an answer, get where we're going, go somewhere new.

the3rdthing.press